Director of production
SUSAN. M. MOYER

Developmental editor
GABE A. ROSEN

Book design, senior project manager
JENNIFER L. POLSON

Dust jacket design
JOSEPH BRUMLEVE

Photo imaging
TRACY GAUDREAU AND
JOSEPH BRUMLEVE

Copy editor
CYNTHIA L. McNEW

ISBN 1-58261-679-5

Printed in the United States.

This book is dedicated to my wife
Courtney: My inspiration, my hero and
my "gooser."

You always have the words to lift me up,
and I love you for that.

•••

To Mom and Dad:
Your love is unconditional
and support endless.
Thank you.

ACKNOWLEDGMENTS

When I sat in Sports Publishing's break room in Champaign, Illinois sharing popcorn and a Diet Coke with Sports Publishing's director of acquisitions Scott Rauguth, I asked if he really knew what he was getting into with a book about a Latin superstar. He said he didn't. "And," he said, "that's what makes what we're doing exciting." Thanks to Scott and Erin Linden-Levy for believing in and fighting for the project.

A big thank you to Dean Reinke, who thought it would be a good idea for Scott to meet this Spanish-speaking sportswriter he knew.

When I decided to write this book, I didn't really know where to start. The person I turned to is the person I always turn to when I need help on a project. Thanks to Ted Gangi, one of my best friends and the best sports mind I've ever met. You're the best!

Thanks to Enrique Rojas of ESPNDeportes.com and the *Hoy* newspaper in Santo Domingo, Dominican Republic. Enrique took in a stranger he knew only by e-mail and telephone and gave selflessly of his time and knowledge. Without Enrique's insistence that I *had* to see certain things, this project would have never happened.

Thanks to Doña Andrea Soriano for graciously opening her home and sharing her time. Thanks to Angel "Aroboy" Santana for the insight, suggestions and assistance in San Pedro de Macoris.

Thanks to media relations directors Rick Cerrone of the New York Yankees, Kevin Shea of the Boston Red Sox, Jay Horowitz and Shannon Dalton of the New York Mets, Monique Giroux of the Montreal Expos and John Blake and his Texas Rangers staff.

A big "thank you" to Mitsunori Ueno, Tatsuma Kajiguchi and the staff at the Hiroshima Toyo Carp Academy and to Eledoro R. Arias and the staff of the Los Angeles Dodgers' Campo Las Palmas. A "thanks" to my boys at the Hotel Delta in Santo Domingo and to Franklyn Mirabel, sports editor of *Hoy*.

Thanks to Victor Andriani, Pastor Ayala, Marty "Coach" Garza, Bonnie Greenslade, Mike Hashimoto, Ryan Horton, Hollis Jackson, Josh Lewin, Court Loeffler, Mike Martin, Jon Rahoi and Keith Whitmire for listening and to Steve Richardson for being my mentor.

Thanks to *The Dallas Morning News*, John Banks, Ivan Sokalsky and Carlos Coban of ESPNDeportes.com for pointing me in the right direction.

Thanks to Keenan Delaney, Michael Westbay of JapaneseBaseball.com and Gary Aladdin of BaseballGuru.com.

Thank to Dave Campbell, Roberto Clemente Jr., Chuck Cooperstein, Ken Daley, Peter Gammons, Evan Grant, Mr. and Mrs. Trey Hillman, Bob Horner, Michael Kay, Tim Kurkjian, Omar Minaya, Willie Randolph, Mike Rhyner and Greg Williams of "The Hardline," Robert Whiting, and to players Roberto Alomar, Shea Hillenbrand, Barry Larkin, Pedro Martinez, Raul Mondesi, Jose Offerman, Tomo Ohka, Andy Pettite, Timo Perez, Mariano Rivera, Fernando Tatis and Bernie Williams.

A special thanks to my family: Kelsey Monk, LB and Elizabeth Monk, Gary and Sandy Mossman, Brett and Jennifer Mossman, Ryan and Sydni Mossman, Prof and Jo Patrick, Todd, Leslie and Olivia Reves.

Thanks for the encouragement!

CONTENTS

Simply put, Alfonso Soriano had one of the most amazing offensive years in baseball history in 2002. The New York Yankees' leadoff man hit 39 home runs, stole 41 bases and finished third in the American League MVP voting.

He broke the American League record for home runs by a second baseman and became the first second baseman to join the 30-30 club and only the third middle infielder, joining Texas Rangers shortstop Alex Rodriguez and Cincinnati Reds shortstop Barry Larkin, in the prestigious club. Soriano finished in the top five among American League leaders in home runs, doubles and total bases. He led the league in hits, runs, at-bats, stolen bases and extra-base hits—all in only his second full major-league season.

Soriano did it all—and continues to do it all—with a style and charisma that teammate Bernie Williams describe as "contagious." Though his hometown of San Pedro de Macoris has seen its share of players (the town has produced over 60 major-league players), Soriano, because of his personality and constant smile, has endeared himself to his country and hometown as much, if not more, than any other current player.

However, Soriano's journey to the steps of the 40-40 club was neither typical nor ideal. He originally signed with the Hiroshima Toyo Carp of the Japanese league. After spending most of three years in the Japanese minor leagues, Soriano took almost a complete year off before resurfacing with the Yankees in the fall of 1998.

Featuring interviews with current and former players, broadcasters and those who know Soriano best, *Alfonso Soriano: The Dominican Dream Come True* takes a detailed look at that journey, analyzes his season from a historical standpoint and takes a look at what's in store for one of baseball's brightest stars.

Of the 849 players on 2002 Opening Day major-league rosters, 222 were born outside the United States. Only 27 of those 222 were not of Latin American origin. And that number is only going to increase, with almost 50 percent of minor-league players born outside the United States.

The Latin player is also gaining in status. Of the players on *The Sporting News* Top 50 Players list, 19 were from Spanish-speaking countries, including reigning American League MVP Miguel Tejada of the Oakland A's.

With his status, Soriano has the chance to impact as many Latinos in New York as he does in the Dominican Republic. In New York City, Latinos are more than 2.1 million of the city's eight million citizens. Puerto Ricans and Dominicans account for almost half of the 2.1 million.

That percentage is almost identical on major-league rosters, where Puerto Ricans and Dominicans account for 112 of the 222 foreign-born players, with the Dominican Republic boasting 74 of the 112.

Soriano used to be like any of the other thousands of kids I saw running around Parque Olímpico, any number of barrios in San Pedro de Macoris and even the pristine major-league academies like the Los Angeles Dodgers' Campo Las Palmas.

The young players are playing to impress, but they are also playing because their passion is unyielding. Some may describe this passion as a way out of a poor country, and it can be exactly that. But these players don't see the game as a payday waiting to happen. They see it as a way to make a living doing what they love—a way to help their family "earn our daily food." Every day they are still in the game and still able to contribute to their families, they give thanks. Among Latin players, not even the next day is taken for granted. When talking about what kind of numbers a player expects to have or what kind of year his team may have, a Latino player will often qualify predictions with *si Dios quiere* or God willing.

"How many home runs will you hit this year?"

"Maybe 30, *si Dios quiere*."

"Can you guys finish first in the AL East?"

"If we get good pitching and *si Dios quiere*."

It even overflows to the streets of cities like Santo Domingo and San Pedro de Macoris. While swapping stories with a 16-year-old prospect over freshly squeezed orange juice in Santo Domingo, I asked if he thought he would be signed by the time I came back next year: "I think I'll be playing with someone—*si Dios quiere*."

Each day *Dios* provides the opportunity to play is yet other day for opportunity—for the player to earn his *comida* and for him to do what he loves to do.

The Latin passion for baseball not only runs deep, it's entrenched in the culture. In the Dominican Republic, the game's influence is simply a part of life. Its influences are felt in the fruit markets, on any street corner and in almost any conversation.

Soriano made his name a big part of those conversations after a magical year, and you can expect it to remain right there for a long time.

Cody Monk
March 2003

ALFONSO SORIANO

THE DOMINICAN DREAM COME TRUE

1

Welcome to the
Big Time, Kid

It was controlled anarchy in the Quisqueya barrio of San Pedro de Macoris, and Andrea Soriano needed time to herself. She took a deep breath and exchanged pleasantries with the crowd gathering in her own home. There were friends, family and other San Pedro de Macoris residents who might as well be family. She escaped and went looking for a quiet corner on streets only slightly more crowded than her living room.

The humid, salty Dominican Republic night was much better company at that moment than anyone or anything going on in a country where baseball and the trials and travails of the United States dollar dominate news.

Mrs. Soriano could slip unnoticed into another neighborhood or nearby park and watch children use anything straight and solid to hit anything pitched, round and reasonably visible. No, that would be too much of a reminder.

She could knock on almost any door in this coastal town on the Iguamo River and be greeted with a smile and an offer of drink and conversation. No, not an option.

Every one of the city's 200,000 residents knew what was going on November 4, 2001. She couldn't escape the talk.

Mrs. Soriano needed to be far enough away from the television that she couldn't hear what was being said. Someone could eventually tell her what happened. She might see a replay. Or, she might never see— or want to see—what was going on 2,800 miles away in Phoenix, Arizona.

Maybe she would walk the quarter-mile from her house to the San Pedro de Macoris "Malecón." There, on the seafront avenue, she could find a bench and enjoy, in peace, the million-dollar views of the Caribbean Sea that are a dime a dozen in these parts. No, that wouldn't work either. She didn't want to be that far away. Just in case.

Just in case her son, Alfonso, the New York Yankees' rookie second baseman, was more than just another character in a scene that seemed twisted and out of place.

It was Game 7 of the 2001 World Series. The Arizona Diamondbacks, a team playing its fourth season ever, had pushed Major League Baseball's marquee franchise to a Game 7, using the dominating arms of Randy Johnson and Curt Schilling.

Starting his third game of the series, Schilling was cruising. He had already pitched 21 innings in the series and struck out 26 Yankees. He had issued only two walks and given up three earned runs. The new kids were doing more than trying to get noticed. Arizona was standing toe to toe with an organization playing in its 38th World Series and looking for it 27th world championship.

To sip the champagne again, the Yankees would need heroics from the wiry second baseman with the oversized bat. The one who was pretty sure he had heard of Babe Ruth. The one who knew about Reggie Jackson only because his mom watched Mr. October when she was young. For heroics to happen, Soriano would need his 180-pound body and 34-ounce bat to turn on Schilling, one of the nastiest flamethrowers and split-finger pitchers of this generation. And these heroics would have to come in the pressure of a World Series Game 7 with the score tied 1-1 in the eighth inning.

In the seventh, the Yankees finally tied the game. Derek Jeter broke Schilling's streak of 16 straight retired batters with a single. Jeter came around after Paul O'Neill and Tino Martinez delivered consecutive hits. In the bottom of the seventh, Arizona manager Bob Brenly let Schilling hit instead of turning the game over to a bullpen that had been shaken by Yankee mystique in the ninth innings of Game 4 and Game 5.

x

LEFT: Alfonso is congratulated by Scott Brosius.

When Schilling came out for the eighth inning, the already strange stage turned stranger. With Schilling throwing his final warmup tosses to catcher Damian Miller, a sudden breeze picked up in Phoenix's Bank One Ballpark. Light rain began to fall in the Arizona desert, sending a crowd accustomed to seeing water only in the swimming pool beyond the right center field wall scurrying for umbrellas. When a single food wrapper appeared from the stands and began flying effortlessly over the field and hovering in the outfield just beyond second base, FOX broadcaster Joe Buck wondered along with anyone else watching.

"The wind is starting to pick up," Buck said. "I'm not sure where that came from."

Welcome to the sublime, Joe—probably yet another Yankees ambush laying in wait.

Standing in the on-deck circle watching Schilling warm up, Soriano adjusted the shin guard on his left leg. He walked to the right side of the batter's box to play his part in the ever-unfolding tale.

The veteran Schilling didn't waste time. The rookie had ended Game 5 with a 12th-inning single three innings after Scott Brosius tied it for the Yankees with a two-out, ninth-inning home run, the second straight night New York had been down to its final out before tying the game. Schilling didn't want to put his team in yet another heartbreaking situation.

BELOW: Andrea Soriano outside the entrance to a house Alfonso built.

Courtesy of Cody Monk

Two quick fastballs, and Soriano was behind 0-2. He appeared destined to be Schilling's 10th strikeout victim of the night.

After the second pitch, Andrea Soriano stood and rubbed her temples. She headed for the front door and the peacefulness of the Dominican night.

"I was afraid he was going to strike out," Andrea Soriano said. "When Alfonso gets two strikes on him, no matter what game he's playing or what pitcher he's playing against, I don't watch, I just turn my back and don't watch because I don't want to see him strike out. I don't want to see him feeling like he's failed. In that game when he got those two strikes, I got as far away as I could."

While his mother ducked away from the home they share, Soriano dug in against a pitcher who went 22-6 with a 2.98 ERA and 293 strikeouts. Schilling threw his trademark split-finger. Soriano fouled it off. Back to the fastball—Soriano just got a piece of it.

The Arizona crowd now standing, Miller called for a fastball away. Schilling shook his head, wanting to finish Soriano with another split-finger. The pitch dove away from Soriano around ankle level and quickly headed toward the dirt.

Soriano wound the huge bat like a driver. He put his strong forearms and quick

wrists into the swing and made contact. This time, he didn't just get a piece of the ball. He got all of the ball. And in the same instant, he broke the collective hearts of the Diamondbacks and their fans.

The ball sailed deep into the left field seats. Left fielder Luis Gonzalez gave the smash only a brief look.

As soon as he hit the ball, Soriano tossed his bat aside and allowed himself to watch…for a moment. In Game 1 of the American League Championship Series against Seattle, Soriano hit a ball he thought was gone. He stood at the plate admiring the shot. When the ball bounced off the wall and Soriano was held to a single, manager Joe Torre gave him a thorough tongue-lashing. This time, he could admire all he wanted. Only a fan was getting to this ball. As he touched first, coach Lee Mazzilli gave Soriano a congratulatory tap and then allowed himself a quick celebration.

Soriano rounded first, leaned to his left and threw his right arm in the air, his fist symbolic of the knockout punch most figured he had just delivered.

"I was crushed when he hit it," Schilling said after the game, "because I thought it was a good pitch."

Brenly was just as much in disbelief. He saw Miller bend down to make the stop on a pitch Brenly said "nearly bounced in

Soriano avoids a sliding Shannon Stewart.

AP/WWP

the dirt. And [Soriano] just golfed it out of there."

"I was simply trying to make good contact on a pitch, being that I was the leadoff guy," Soriano told the New York *Daily News*, "just trying to get on base."

Instead, Soriano circled the bases and gave the Yankees a 2-1 lead with Mariano Rivera lurking in the bullpen. The home run was a needed lift for a team that hit .183 and scored only 14 runs in the seven-game series. When Soriano reached third, coach Willie Randolph offered a handshake and smile. Without Randolph's tutoring and demands that the team stay patient with the ultra-talented second baseman during the year, Soriano could well have been watching 2001 from the bench—or from the Triple-A Columbus Clippers' bench.

"When [Soriano] hit that home run," Gonzalez said later, "you could just feel the air being let out of our stadium. Our fans just got quiet."

In San Pedro de Macoris, the controlled anarchy turned to mayhem—both in the streets and in the Soriano house. Andrea Soriano's need for refuge quickly turned to a need to know. Her first thought, as it always is: "Was he okay? What happened? Did Alfonso get a hit? Did he strike out?"

One of Soriano's best friends, Angel Santana, a Los Angeles Dodgers scout known in the Dominican simply as "Aroboy," found Andrea and told her she needed to get back in the house.

"I didn't know what he had done," Andrea Soriano said. "I didn't see the actual home run. I only saw it on replays. I knew he could do something like that, but I really thought he was going to strike out."

"I was at [the Soriano] house," Santana said, "and not long after he hit the home run I looked at my cell phone, and I had 12 messages on it from people just screaming and talking about the home run. The same thing was going on in the streets. People everywhere were going crazy."

Soriano raised his right arm again as he crossed the plate. This time he left the hand open, leaving it available for congratulations from Brosius and David Justice, the two batters after him. Jeter welcomed Soriano to a dugout feeling confident a fourth straight title was headed their way. And why not? Soriano had given the Yankees a 2-1 lead, and Rivera, a closer with 23 straight postseason saves, was warming for the bottom of the inning.

"We had been fighting them tooth and nail the whole series," Yankees center fielder Bernie Williams said.

Alfonso is greeted at the plate by Derek Jeter (left), catcher Jorge Posada (right), and the rest of the team after hitting a home-run in Game 7 of the 2001 World Series.

AP/WWP

"And then all of the sudden he comes up with that home run. At that point we're thinking we like our chances with one of the best closers ever coming in."

Schilling stepped off the mound and took another ball from home plate umpire Steve Rippley. He stood to the left of the mound looking toward the outfield. He put the ball, his glove and his hat in his left hand and slicked his blonde hair back with his right while looking at Gonzalez, Steve Finley and Danny Bautista gathered in center field.

"We saw who was warming up out there," Finley said after the game.

As the Diamondbacks' outfielders talked, Brenly walked to the mound and took Schilling out of the game. Soriano, the rookie, had knocked out Schilling, the superstar.

When Rivera struck out the side in the eighth, Soriano was poised to put a World Series MVP trophy alongside his memorable home run. Before the home run and his Game 5-ending single in the 12th inning, Soriano had kept the Yankees in the Series with his defense, something questioned coming into the year.

In Game 2, Arizona led 1-0 in the bottom of the second and was threatening to give starter Randy Johnson even more. With Bautista on third, Mark Grace hit a bouncer to Soriano, who was playing just off the infield grass. Bautista broke for the plate on contact and, after Soriano juggled the ball, looked like he would score easily. Soriano collected himself after the bobble and threw a laser to catcher Jorge Posada to get his countryman Bautista at home.

With the game tied 1-1 in the sixth inning of Game 3, Reggie Sanders was on second when Erubiel Durazo hit a sharp grounder up the middle. Soriano made a diving stop to keep the ball from getting to the outfield. His throw drew Tino Martinez off the first base bag, but Sanders didn't score. The Yankees ended up winning 2-1, their first win of the Series.

A game later, Soriano made sure Yankees fans saw their team go 3-0 in Series games at Yankee Stadium. Brosius tied the game in the ninth with the first of New York's two dramatic home runs off Byung-Hyun Kim. With one out in the 11th, Arizona loaded the bases with Rivera on the mound and Sanders batting. Rivera threw Sanders an 0-2, cut fastball on the outside edge of the plate. Sanders hit it off the end of the bat and up the middle. Soriano, who had cheated toward second before the pitch, dove for Sanders's liner. He nabbed it with the ball hitting the edge of the webbing in his glove. The defensive gem set up Soriano's 12th-inning single, an opposite-field liner

that Sanders fielded cleanly. When the throw short-hopped catcher Rod Barajas and allowed Chuck Knoblauch to score, Soriano had a game-winning hit. And more than one Diamondbacks player was left wondering if there really was something to the legend of Yankee Stadium.

"[Soriano's] play just took the heart out of me," Sanders said afterward. "At that point I'm thinking, 'What's up with this Yankee Stadium?'"

Soriano didn't win the Series MVP. That went to Schilling and Johnson after Rivera blew his first postseason save in four years. However, the Game 7 home run and the game winner he hit against Seattle closer Kazuhiro Sasaki in Game 4 of the American League Championship Series in Yankee Stadium served notice that the slender rookie with the heavy bat was about to be a major force for a long time in the Bronx.

"That World Series was almost like his personal resume tape," Yankees television play-by-play voice Michael Kay said. "He has unbelievable strength, and he did it on an unbelievably big stage in the World Series. He was showcasing in [Game 7] everything the Yankees thought he was going to be."

Even before the home run, Soriano had shown the organization plenty to be excited about. He finished third in the Rookie of the Year voting behind the Mariners' Ichiro

Suzuki and C.C. Sabathia of Cleveland. Batting in the ninth spot, Soriano hit 18 home runs and had 73 RBIs and 43 stolen bases. Only Tommie Agee, who had 22 home runs and 44 stolen bases for the White Sox in 1966, had a rookie year with more homers and steals.

"The guy has lightning in his bat," Yankees pitcher Andy Pettite said. "It's funny because you see this little bitty guy with this big bat. But he's got these quick wrists and then you realize how much power he can really produce."

"I remember watching TV when he hit that home run," said Trey Hillman, Soriano's manager during Soriano's two years at Triple-A Columbus and a coach with Grand Canyon in the Arizona Fall League where Soriano played in 1998. "It didn't surprise me. Not that I had seen him do something like that a bunch. It's just that I can't allow myself to be surprised any more by anything he does."

After the 2001 World Series, Soriano, like he does every winter, returned to San Pedro de Macoris. Even though New York had lost, his star was even bigger with his San Pedro de Macoris friends and family. There was a proclamation from the president of the Dominican Republic. There was a plaque honoring Soriano as an outstanding citizen in the San Pedro de Macoris

OPPOSITE: Alfonso collides with Reds catcher Jason LaRue during a 2003 interleague matchup.

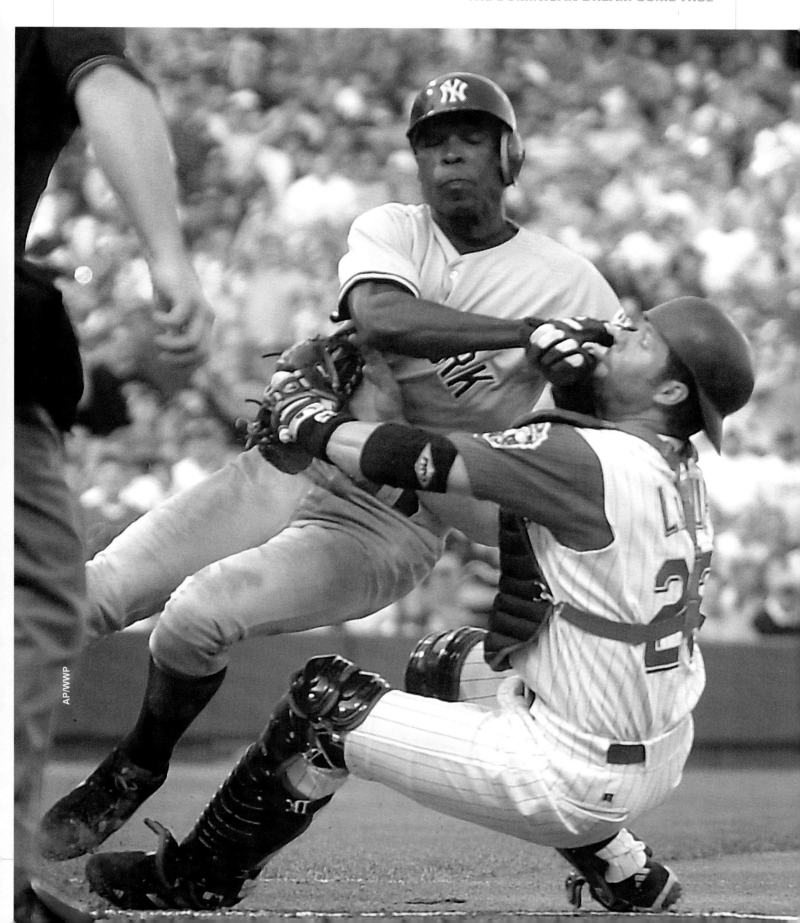

winter, when the Dominican Republic is an hour ahead of New York time, she likely had called while he was asleep.

When he saw he had more than 10 messages before 10 a.m., he immediately thought something was wrong. He listened to the messages, three of which were from his mother, who was crying and wanting to know, as always, if he was okay. Soriano flipped on the television and began dialing his home number in the Dominican Republic.

The almost constant smile on Soriano's face turned to disbelief when he saw flames coming from the Belle Harbor neighborhood in Queens. His body shivered with chills when he saw the cause of the flames. American Airlines flight 587 from New York's John F. Kennedy Airport to Las Americas Airport in Santo Domingo had crashed shortly after takeoff, killing all 260 passengers and crew on board and five more on the ground. When his mother picked up the phone, she started crying again. The youngest of her four children was fine. Despite rumors floating from several Spanish-language media outlets in New York, Soriano hadn't switched his scheduled November 16 departure. "I thanked God when he called me back," Andrea Soriano said. "I knew about his schedule, but I was thinking about him when I heard the news.

God has blessed me with Alfonso, and I just wanted to make sure he was okay."

Soriano was not on the flight, but both he and his mother were certain they knew someone who was. Soon the victims began being identified. An acquaintance from San Pedro de Macoris was on the flight. So was the mother of former major-league pitcher Yorkis Perez.

Enrique Rojas is a columnist for the daily *Hoy* newspaper in Santo Domingo. He also has a weeknight baseball television talk show and is considered an authority on Dominican baseball. He said the accident sent shock waves all over the island, including the baseball community.

"What a lot of people don't understand about the Dominican Republic is that it's a populous country [7.8 million], but it seems like everyone knows everyone, and everyone acts that way," Rojas said. "Yorkis Perez lost his mother, but there were a lot of worried players at that time. Most of those that come home to play winter ball were already here, but players were worried about friends, family. After that happened, that's all anyone talked about, ballplayer or not, for a long time, because almost anyone you talked to was affected by it in some way."

The accident took such a toll on the country because of the number of Dominicans living in New York and the

OPPOSITE: Alfonso acknowledges the crowd while playing for the Estrellas del Oriente in the Dominican Republic Winter Leagues.

number who normally make the 1,550-mile, one-way commute. According to the 2000 census, almost 407,000 Dominicans call New York home. After the census numbers were released, several politicians said the numbers weren't accurate and that the city miscalculated by almost 200,000 people, a number that would have put Dominicans alongside Puerto Ricans as New York's largest Latino minority group. While most congregate in Manhattan's Washington Heights neighborhood, Dominicans are starting to spread out, especially in the Bronx and Queens, where the crash happened.

The accident was almost two months to the day after the September 11, 2001 terrorist attacks. The world, nation, and New York City especially were on high alert. Tensions were still high about traveling in general. The National Transportation Safety Board declared the crash an accident due to "wake turbulence caused after the takeoff of a [Japan Airlines] 747 on runway 31 left" that caused the entire vertical tail fin to separate and both engines to come apart from the wings. The engines landed 100 feet from one another near Newport Avenue and Beach 129th Street. The aircraft's body crashed not far away on Beach 131st Street in a residential neighborhood.

Alfonso and Orioles catcher Benji Gil share a moment of silence in memory of the 9/11 attacks.

Soriano assured his mother he was fine and would see her soon. Soriano then started returning calls to the litany of friends who had also called wondering about his whereabouts. He then began thinking about how the crash would affect his winter stay in San Pedro de Macoris. He was coming

AP/WWP

off a rookie season that had the Yankees thinking they had found their second baseman of the future. He would play in the Dominican Winter Leagues' round-robin playoffs with the Estrellas Orientales and his friend Vladimir Guerrero of the Montreal Expos. However, Soriano knew those plaques in his house would make him someone the community would turn to for assistance.

"I know that when I get back to the Dominican Republic a lot of people will come to me and ask for help," Soriano told *The New York Times*. "If I can help them, I will help them."

Providing that help began with the Dominican community in New York. He used the time at Gallagher's, where he was supposed to be promoting a new lunch menu, to announce he would have a dinner at the steakhouse for the victims' families the following spring.

When he got home, the swarm did follow. He got noticed more than he had in the past. With most people trying to put the crash behind them, the talk turned to his season and, specifically, his Game 7 home run. People also wanted to know when he was going to start playing.

Teams in the Dominican Winter Leagues play a 50-game season. The top four teams in the six-team league advance to an 18-game, round-robin playoff series. Each

team plays nine games at home and nine away. The two teams with the best record after the round-robin play a best-of-seven series to determine the league's entry in the Caribbean Series. The highly competitive league is littered with major leaguers. And when the playoffs start, even more big-league players join the fun. The league is like a pickup basketball game between friends. Every once in a while, an outsider (for example, a foreign player whom a major league club wants to have more experience) slides in. For the most part, players play on teams close to where they grew up or currently live. Most have known each other for years. Often, players who just battled each other in the major-league playoffs are laughing and joking and battling other acquaintances as winter-league teammates.

In the Dominican Winter Leagues, the best player among the group doesn't always play. He picks his spots and normally waits for the most competitive games. And down there, the most competitive games are the playoffs and the eventual Caribbean Series. Soriano joined the Estrellas for their playoff run in early 2002. That same playoff season, Bartolo Colon of the Chicago White Sox, the Dodgers' Odalis Perez, Julio Franco of the Atlanta Braves, Raul Mondesi of the New York Yankees and reigning American League MVP Miguel Tejada were among the current

OPPOSITE: Alfonso connects for his first big-league hit.

or former major-league All-Stars who played in the 2002 Dominican Winter League playoffs that January.

Soriano wanted to use the time to better his plate discipline (he struck out 125 times and drew only 29 walks his first year) and continue adjusting to second. He played in all 18 Estrellas playoff games, hitting seventh for a team that did not advance to the final series. In 77 at-bats, he hit .325 with two home runs and 11 RBIs and scored 11 runs. Being more selective was still a work a progress, as he only had two walks and struck out 18 times.

The time with the Estrellas readied Soriano for a spring training where despite having a solid 2001, he knew he needed to convince the Yankees that defensively, he had truly made the switch from natural shortstop to second baseman. In 2001, Soriano tied Jerry Hairston Jr. of the Baltimore Orioles with 19 errors for the major-league lead among second basemen—a total that also put both in the top eight in the majors for any position player.

"Just because you play second base doesn't mean you're a second baseman," said Yankees third base coach and six-time All-Star second baseman Willie Randolph, who has played more games at second (1,688) than any other Yankee. "[During that year's spring training], we were still in the beginning phases of him learning the position. We're now in phase two or three of getting him to be where he needs to be as far as playing the position goes."

The Yankees turned Randolph loose with Soriano. The team was willing to live with a second baseman-in-training as long as he could produce offensively. Soriano still struggled in the field in 2002, leading major-league second basemen with 23 errors, eight more than any other American League second baseman. To the team, that was like saying the prettiest girl in the school occasionally has a bad hair day.

At the Yankees' spring training complex at Legends Field in Tampa, a Ralph Waldo Emerson quote greets visitors on the wall opposite the entrance to the hall that leads to the clubhouse. "Don't go where the path may lead," Emerson wrote. "Go instead where there is no path and leave a trail."

The home run off Schilling started Soriano down that path not yet taken. Spring training 2002 sent him blazing down a trail that would see him produce one of the most amazing offensive years ever for a second baseman. He joined elite company. He broke records. He set new offensive standards for second basemen. He was one home run short of becoming only the fourth member ever in the 40-40 club. Soriano was creating a new path, all right. But it is hard to say he

left a trail, because some of the standards—joining the 30-30 club—had never been reached by any second baseman. And he set marks that may never be reached again.

Soriano began the magical journey with a spring that turned any head associated with the Yankees. Playing in 26 of the team's 34 spring games, he had 29 hits and 43 total bases. The 29 hits were the third most of any player in baseball that spring. Among Yankees, shortstop Derek Jeter was a distant second with 24 hits and designated hitter-first baseman Nick Johnson followed Soriano with 39 total bases. Soriano tied Johnson for the team lead in runs (16). Soriano also finished tied for third in RBIs with 12. Since

manager Joe Torre was toying with the idea of letting Soriano hit leadoff during the season, the second baseman led the team with 96 at-bats. Johnson and outfielder Shane Spencer were the only other Yankees with more than 63 at-bats that spring.

The torrid run through spring training had Soriano in the Opening Day lineup, hitting leadoff and playing second base in a 10-3 loss at Baltimore. Soriano didn't get a hit that day, but it seemed like he did almost every other day in April. For the month, he had 14 multi-hit games, including his first five-hit game April 8 in a 16-3 win at Toronto. That day he had a double and his second stolen base of the year and he belted a three-run homer.

Three days later, Soriano started a 10-game hitting streak stretching from April 11 to 21. Only the April 15 game against Boston and the April 20 game against Toronto weren't multiple-hit games. Dating back to April 7, Soriano had at least two hits in 11 of 14 games. The day before the hitting streak started was the only game in that run where he didn't have a hit.

By April 21, Soriano was hitting .395 and slugging .663. He was already leading the league in hits, multihit games, extra-base hits and total bases. For the month of April, he hit .348 and had 40 hits in 26 games. His only disappointment in the season's first month came when he didn't see his name in the lineup April 13 at Fenway Park against the Boston Red Sox. It was the only game of the month he didn't play. Torre told Soriano he was sitting down because of a sore left hamstring. Soriano sat on the bench, but he didn't like it, especially since fellow Dominican Pedro Martinez was on the mound. Soriano knew his cell phone would ring after the game with friends from the Dominican wondering why he didn't face Pedro.

"When Pedro pitches," said Angel Santana, a Los Angeles Dodgers scout in San Pedro de Macoris and one of Soriano's best friends, "the streets in the Dominican are filled with people. Soriano is competitive, and he knows what it's like down here when Pedro pitches."

Soriano wasted little time keeping his April streak going. After home runs in the first and second innings against Tampa Bay on May 8, he started thinking about another recent accomplishment.

After the game, Soriano said that after his second home run he told his teammates that he wanted to "try to do the same thing Mike Cameron did." What Cameron did six

AP/WWP

days earlier was hit four home runs against the Chicago White Sox. What Soriano was doing was starting to pop up on radar screens around the league.

"Playing in Toronto, I hadn't heard much about him other than he was a hard worker," said Raul Mondesi who became a teammate of Soriano's after a July 1 trade. "But then it was like you started hearing all of the sudden about what he was doing, the home runs, the offensive production from second base the Yankees were getting."

After the two-home run game against the Devil Rays, Soriano went without a home run or RBI in the next five games. He broke out of the slump May 16 at home against Tampa Bay with a solo home run. When the Twins rolled in for a weekend series a day later, Soriano greeted them with two homers and six RBIs in the first two games.

The second game was a snapshot of Soriano's season thus far. He struck out in his first three at-bats against Tony Fiore. With two on and the scored tied 2-2 in the sixth, Bob Wells relieved Fiore. Soriano then got a 2-0 fastball up in the zone. He drove it out for his team-leading 11th home run and a 5-2 Yankees lead. In his last at-bat, Soriano struck out again, giving him 49 in 42 games.

"[Soriano's] tough to figure out," Torre said after the game. "At this juncture, we're not expecting him to lead the club in home runs. And here he is."

Soriano's postgame explanation was a bit more to the point: "When I see the high ball, I see the ball and I swing," Soriano said.

That aggressiveness, combined with pitchers wanting to get him out so they don't have to face Derek Jeter, Jason Giambi and Bernie Williams with men on base, started rumblings that Soriano could make the All-Star team. Boston Red Sox center fielder Johnny Damon was thinking even bigger after Soriano led off the fifth and sixth innings with home runs in the Yankees' 14-5 win over the Red Sox on May 26 in Fenway Park. The two shots pushed Soriano's total to 14, tying him with Texas Rangers shortstop Alex Rodriguez for the league lead.

"Soriano is the league MVP right now," Damon said afterwards. "You have to get him out, or he's going to score."

Proving both his versatility and the unpredictably Torre had noticed, Soriano's legs were the story in his first trip to Coors Field. In the Yankees' 20-10 win over the Rockies on June 19, Soriano hit his 16th home run of the year, but his consecutive stolen bases in the third inning to give him 19 for the year began the talk that something special was about to happen.

At the All-Star break, Soriano was hitting .315 with 20 home runs and 23 stolen bases. He was voted to the All-Star Game as a starter. As soon as he got the news he would be starting at Miller Park in Milwaukee, he called his mom.

"Alfonso is the kind of person who is always kidding around, especially with me," his mother Andrea Soriano said. "He said, 'Mami, I'm going to the All-Star Game, but there are really only going to be two All-Stars there: me and Barry Bonds.'"

Though he was joking with his mom, Soriano and Bonds were the only ones to hit home runs in a game that will be remembered more for its score (a 7-7 tie) than anything a single player did. Bonds went deep in the third, and Soriano, again shining on the big stage, hit one out in the fifth.

"When I had him in [the Arizona Fall League] in 1998, I started talking with Yankees development people who were asking me where I thought he fit," said Trey Hillman, who also managed Soriano for two years at Triple-A Columbus. "I asked them, 'Where do you want him to fit?' I told them they could put him at catcher or first base or wherever, and he'd be an All-Star in three years. The knucklehead proved me wrong. He was an All-Star in two."

Despite the statistics that already had some talking MVP, one person Soriano passed on every home run trot still wasn't completely impressed. Even though he had 12 errors at the break, he hadn't made one since June 12, almost a month before the All-Star Game. Still, third base coach Willie Randolph thought that was too many.

"Last year he made the All-Star team completely for his hitting," said Randolph. "You're a legit All-Star when you make a team with your defense and you're not even thinking about your offensive game."

The All-Star Game proved to be exactly what Soriano needed. Two games into the second half of the season, against Cleveland, Soriano gave the Yankees a 1-0 lead on the second pitch of the game, his seventh leadoff homer of the year. The next inning, he hit a three-run shot off Indians starter Ryan Drese on a familiar 0-2 count.

That's all Soriano needed to get going again. He homered in three of the next five games, driving in five runs in the stretch. Soriano then started working on his stolen bases, stealing a bag in each of the next four games. The last in that run, on July 27 against Tampa Bay, was his 30th of the season. At the time, he already had 25 home runs, and talk began of Soriano joining Bobby Bonds as the only Yankees in the 30-30 club. If Soriano did hit five more home runs, he would be the only second baseman ever to join the 30-30 club.

On August 11, the possibility turned to probability after Soriano took A's pitcher Mark Mulder deep in a three-hit, three-run performance in an 8-5 win. Five games later

on a Saturday night in Seattle, the time came to etch Soriano's name into the record books. In the seventh, he smacked a James Baldwin fastball for his 30th home run of the year. His legs not wanting to be outdone, he also stole his 34th base, prompting even more talk.

"That guy's awesome. He could go 40-40," Yankees center fielder Bernie Williams said, immediately beginning talk about the feat being a real possibility.

Torre added: "We don't know what the ceiling is for this kid."

Despite the accolades from his manager and teammates, Soriano wanted everyone to hold up a minute.

"I don't want to even think about it," Soriano said after being told of Williams's comments and the SORIANO 30-30 T-shirts several teammates were sporting in the clubhouse.

"I had to play five or six more games to get my 30th, so I don't want to think about 40-40."

He might not have been thinking about it, but Soriano wouldn't let anyone stop talking about it. He did go a week without a homer after getting No. 30. Then came another one of those hot streaks. He hit four home runs in the next five games to raise his total to 34. He capped the run with a two-homer game on August 30 in a win over Toronto, a game in which he also stole his 36th base.

to make a run at 40. Rodriguez stole his 30th base in his 107th game, two games before Larkin; Soriano stole base No. 30 in Game 102. While Soriano was ahead of Rodriguez's steal totals, Rodriguez started eyeing 40 home runs 22 games before Soriano. Even though he finished with 42 home runs and 46 stolen bases, Rodriguez needed almost every remaining game to get to 40-40. He went 13 games between home runs 36 and 37. And Rodriguez needed 11 games between his 39th and 40th, the same number Soriano had left when he got his 39th.

Like Soriano, Rodriguez was still hitting while trying to go from 30 to 40 homers. In the 41 games between his 30th and 39th home runs, Soriano hit over .300. In the 54 games it took Rodriguez to get from 30 to 40, he hit .311 with 22 multiple-hit games.

While there was almost no chance of Larkin getting the 10 home runs in eight games he needed to make 40-40 (Larkin did hit two homers on the last day of the season to push his total to 33), he could have made a run at the 40-steal mark. He stole his 36th base in the 138th game of the season and then didn't steal another base the rest of the year.

"When I had 28 home runs I remember thinking, 'Oh my goodness, I can do this,'" Larkin said. "There was more pressure for me when I was trying to go from 49 to 50 stolen bases [the year before]. I never

expected to hit home runs. I didn't feel that much pressure [to get to 30-30], but there was a period late in the season where I was trying to lift the ball. I'm sure Soriano felt the same way."

Larkin said the situation the Reds and Yankees were in during the 30-30 years affected his approach and likely Soriano's. Because New York plays a team-first style under Torre, Soriano didn't have to bear the brunt of the offensive load like Larkin, who was coming off an MVP year in 1995.

"I was surrounded by a lot of good players, but I hit second or third almost all year," Larkin said. "I remember a lot of times going up there and laying down a bunt to move a guy over. When I got close, a lot of people said to me: 'Expand your strike zone.' I got my 30th with about two weeks left in the season. There was a lot of media and attention on it. In Soriano's case, he's a leadoff man, and pitchers want to get him out because they don't want to face Jeter, Giambi. But over there they've got people who are expected to do things. Giambi and Jeter and all those stud pitchers are expected to win games. Soriano, being a leadoff man, doesn't always get the headlines. But he showed how integral a part of the team they are."

Before Soriano, former Chicago Cub Ryne Sandberg, former Phillie and Met and San Pedro de Macoris native Juan Samuel, Dodgers and A's great Davey Lopes and Hall of Famer and former Cincinnati Red Joe Morgan were the only second basemen to get close to the 30-30 Soriano accomplished in 121 games.

In 1973, Morgan had 26 home runs and 67 steals. He had 27 home runs and 60 stolen bases in his MVP year of 1976. Samuel had 28 home runs, 100 RBIs and 35 steals in 1987. Lopes stole more than 40 bases seven times, but never hit more than 28 homers. Only Sandberg stayed with Soriano on the power scale, hitting 40 homers and stealing 25 bases in 1990.

Simply put, no other second baseman has ever had a season like Soriano's 2002. He finished third in the Most Valuable Player voting behind countryman, winter league foe and Oakland A's shortstop Miguel Tejada and Texas Rangers shortstop Alex Rodriguez.

With 39 home runs, Soriano broke the American League record for homers by a second baseman and was three away from Davey Johnson and Rogers Hornsby's major league record. He led the major leagues in hits (209), runs (128) and at-bats. His 696 at-bats set a Yankees record, were the most by any major-league player in 18 years and were only nine away from former Kansas City Royal Willie Wilson's all-time record.

Soriano was second in the majors in total bases (381). His 41 stolen bases topped the American League and were fourth overall. The 39 home runs put him fifth in the American League. Soriano also finished third in the league with 51 doubles, the third most by any Yankees player and the most since Lou Gehrig had 52 in 1927. His 99 RBIs as a leadoff man (two RBIs came hitting ninth and one while batting third) were one short of joining the Angels' Darin Erstad as the only players to ever drive in 100 runs from the leadoff spot.

Soriano also continued to perform in pressure situations. He hit .329 with runners in scoring position. Thirteen times he led off an inning with a home run, and 15 of his homers came after falling behind on a first-pitch strike. He did have his share of success against teams like Tampa Bay (.321, four HRs, 14 RBI), but he hit .343 with five home runs, 11 RBIs and nine stolen bases against the rival Red Sox. The nine steals were the most he had against any team, and the Rangers, in half as many at-bats, were the only American League team he had a better average against.

"Soriano is a millionaire in talent," Red Sox pitcher Pedro Martinez said. "And the scary thing is that he's got talent and ability that has yet to be seen. I don't think there's any question that he's going to be a mega-star in this league."

"I can't say whether or not the Japanese system is good," Horner told Whiting. "I just don't understand it."

If Horner, a 28-year-old former major-league All-Star and established veteran, couldn't grasp the Japanese system and its focus on practice and team, how would a skinny, 17-year-old Dominican shortstop taught to make sure he stood out fit in? Alfonso Soriano was about to find out.

•••

In San Pedro de Macoris, there is no option. If you grow up in this town 40 minutes east of Santo Domingo, the Dominican Republic capital, baseball will be part of your life somehow. If you aren't one of the ones signed and shipped to a major-league team's academy, you cheer for the players you grew up with and still hang out with every winter. You talk about the game while buying oranges in the fruit market located on the street that takes visitors off Highway 3 into town. If you wear a hat while working the sugar cane fields that surround the city, you wear a hat with some sort of Major League Baseball logo. Most choose the Chicago Cubs hat because of native son Sammy Sosa. However, there are many logos to choose from if you want to cheer for a team with roots in San Pedro de Macoris. How about the Toronto Blue Jays, where natives Tony Fernandez and George Bell

starred? The Braves are a favorite because of former shortstop Rafael Ramirez and the ageless Julio Franco. Montreal currently has Fernando Tatis, who was born in the city, and Jose Offerman, who lives across from the Sorianos on a street known in San Pedro de Macoris as "Avenida de los Peloteros" or Ballplayer's Avenue. The Expos also have fellow Dominican Vladimir Guerrero, who, like Soriano, fell one home run short of a 40-40 season. The Marlins are popular, with speedy San Pedro de Macoris product Luis Castillo currently playing second.

Ask anyone in town where the best place to watch kids play pickup games, and an argument ensues because everyone has a different opinion. And make no mistake, anyone you ask *will* have an opinion.

Many players from the Dominican Republic come from backgrounds that players from the United States could never understand. As a kid, Sosa roamed the city looking for the most concentrated area of people. More people meant more shoes, increasing the potential that someone needed a shoeshine and increasing the chances that Sosa would eat that day.

Reigning American League MVP Miguel Tejada, the Oakland A's shortstop, grew up in Baní, southwest of Santo Domingo. When Hurricane David hit the country in 1979, his family was homeless for

OPPOSITE: Even the youngest of fans get involved in the cheering and spectacle of pickup games in Santo Domingo's Parque Olímpico.

Courtesy of Cody Monk

The main attraction in any Dominican park.

more than two weeks before settling in a refugee camp with 200 other people until they could find housing. By age 11, Tejada had dropped out of school and was ironing shirts in a garment factory so his family could eat while his mother was away during the week working in a bakery and doing odd jobs in Santo Domingo.

In that regard, Soriano was one of the lucky ones. The youngest of Andrea Soriano's four children, Alfonso didn't go hungry or have to drop out of school to make sure the family had plenty. He looked up to his older sister Ambar (33) and his older brothers Julio (31) and Frederico (27). Those two, along with his recently deceased grandfather, were his primary male role models after his parents separated when Alfonso was young. Because she had a young daughter when she got divorced, Andrea moved back in with her parents and promised herself she would never marry again.

"In the Dominican Republic you sometimes hear bad things about stepfathers as it relates to marrying into families with young daughters," Andrea said, leaning forward and erasing, only for a moment, the smile she passed on to her youngest son. "I didn't want any of my kids to have to grow up with a stepfather."

To support her four kids, Andrea cleaned office buildings, did administrative work and other odd jobs around San Pedro de Macoris. As her kids began to get older, she said there were a lot of tough times, but added that she never encountered anything she couldn't handle.

"After I got divorced and decided I wasn't going to get married, God helped me a lot," Andrea said. "He gave me a lot of love. He was always with me. He never gave me any more than I could handle. I worked a lot of different jobs to make sure the kids had what they needed, because I wanted the kids to have a good example."

Minor-league prospects wait for their turn in the cage at Campo Las Palmas, the Dodgers' training facility outside Santo Domingo.

Courtesy of Cody Monk

AP/WWP

The strong will and work ethic Andrea instilled in her kids is particularly evident in Alfonso. Yankees third base coach Willie Randolph said Soriano is a player who "can make light of things you've gotten onto him about. He'll laugh it off, but the next time you see him in the situation you criticized him about, you can see the difference." That desire to get better comes from Andrea's insistence that her kids could always better themselves. Andrea practiced what she preached by often taking on another job or responsibility so her kids had opportunities. She said the sacrifices made the family as tight as they are today. "Alfonso always calls his mother after games," Andrea said.

It wasn't always fun and games in the Soriano household. When school recessed for the summer, the Soriano kids were expected to chip in. They were summoned to their grandfather's farm, where each one had a specific job in the fields. Alfonso's chores consisted of making sure there were no weeds anywhere close to the crops.

"He used to hate going out there to the farm to clear the weeds," Andrea said, smiling. "He would take this stick and walk down the rows. He was always complaining about doing it. It's funny, because Alfonso works hard with everything he does. But he did not like the summers. He was glad to come home and go back to school."

While other kids in San Pedro de Macoris played baseball with makeshift bats, gloves and balls, the Soriano kids were fortunate. Andrea's brother, Hilario, now a Dominican scout for the Blue Jays, had played in the Dodgers' system. When he returned for the winter, he brought whatever equipment he could fit in his bags. From bats and balls to shoes and gloves, if it fit in a duffel bag, Hilario brought it back.

Alfonso got the most use out of Hilario's gifts. Julio and Frederico both played organized baseball, but neither rose above the developmental level.

Alfonso began playing in the same streets and parks that produced Fernandez, Pedro Guerrero, Marion Duncan, Sosa and many others. Like any young Dominican player, he wanted to play shortstop and stand out enough that a scout would recommend him to a major-league club. Through Hilario, the Soriano family knew the Alous, the first family of Dominican baseball. Felipe, now the San Francisco Giants' manager, Matty and Jesus all played at least 15 years in the major leagues. When Alfonso, on January 7, 1994, reached the magical age of 16, the prime time for impressing scouts (Dominican players can sign when they turn 17), the family sought out Jesus both for thoughts and advice. Hilario, then scouting for the Marlins, said he didn't think the club wanted

OPPOSITE: Alfonso avoids the Diamondbacks' Steve Finley and fires the ball to first.

to sign Alfonso, but he wouldn't know for sure until later in the year. Jesus told Alfonso he wanted him to be a pitcher because he was skinny and slow but had a great arm. Alfonso, at the time 5'11" and a whopping 132 pounds, wanted to be "la cabeza," the nickname, meaning "head," for shortstop.

"Looking at him now, you wouldn't believe it, but Alfonso couldn't run back then," said friend Angel Santana. "He had this good arm, but he was running in the 7.0s [in the 60-yard dash]."

In November 1994, less than two months away from his 17th birthday, Soriano was thrown the first curveball of his professional career. Four years earlier, the Hiroshima Toyo Carp of the Japanese Central League opened the gates of a baseball academy much like the ones several major-league clubs were already operating. Late Carp owner Kohei Matsuda put the academy idea in place because importing *gaijin*, like Horner, was becoming more and more expensive. He believed the ratio of production that major-league teams were getting from Latin players to what the players were being paid was high enough to take a crack at bringing Latin players to Japan. The club broke ground on the facility in 1988, the year after Horner's Swallows season, and finished the 270,000-square-meter facility two years later.

The current academy is on the same land, but many of the buildings had to be completely rebuilt after Hurricane George plowed through the Dominican Republic on September 22, 1998. The Carp academy sits on the north side of San Pedro de Macoris. Even with directions and knowing you're on the right road, the place can be hard to find. The manicured entrance is across the road from a gravel parking lot commercial trucks use to either park or make wide turns. The club owns the land on the south side of the entrance but has no plans to do anything with it other than make sure the wild grass doesn't grow out of control.

The entrance is protected by a red sliding gate, and two guards man the lookout booth. One guard is dressed in a white button-down shirt, navy pants and a Carp hat that looks almost identical to a Cincinnati Reds hat. The other guard has on a light brown police uniform that is hardly noticeable next to the machine gun strapped to his shoulder.

A large tree opposite the guard station barely allows enough room to see the sign announcing the academy's existence. Flowers are trimmed just short enough to see the "A" in "Carp" falling off the "ACADEMIA DE BEISBOL; HIROSHIMA TOYO CARP" sign on the brick wall between the security gate and fence that outlines the land.

OPPOSITE: Palm trees and flowers on the grounds of the Carp's academy.

The main office, a two-story building that includes a bathroom with shower, is a quarter-mile drive from the entrance. Team director and scouting chief Mitsunori Ueno, an energetic, diminutive man who laughs when asked if he played the pro game or whether he uses e-mail, sits in an upstairs office with only a map of the academy's grounds and a photo of Matsuda to keep him and the white walls company. Sipping coffee stronger and thicker than the motor oil in the trucks across the road, the 62-year-old Ueno points out the academy's four fields, all of which can be seen from the crow's nest behind each field's home plate. The one on the southeast side is exclusively for batting practice, because the wind coming off the Caribbean Sea blows in the hitter's face, making home runs next to impossible. "I don't need home run hitters. I need contact hitters," Ueno said, reflecting a famous mantra from the Japanese game.

One of the fields has no infield grass, because none of the stadiums in the Japanese major leagues have grass in the infield. Beyond the fence of yet another field, a pack of 20 goats roam freely, with the lone, frustrated handler trying to herd them toward the feeding corrals.

"Investments," says Ueno.

In addition to the goats, the academy churns out prospects that compete in the Dominican Summer League and Instructional Winter League with hopes that some will develop into Japanese major leaguers. On a tour of the facilities, Ueno proudly points out the Dominican Summer League trophy the Carp won last year playing against prospects from major-league clubs. The trophy sits below a 15-foot-long flag that reads ¡*Vamos a Hiroshima, Japón!* (Let's go to Hiroshima, Japan!). Ueno, who has been in the Dominican Republic for more than 40 years, shows off the indoor batting facilities and the group of six pitcher's mounds lined in a row under an overhang. Sixty feet, six inches away and separated by a swath of grass are six batter's stations, also under an overhang. Scattered across the grounds is the academy's, and possibly all of Japanese baseball's, credo: *La práctica hace posible lo imposible* (practice makes the impossible possible).

"One of the things I appreciate most about our facilities is when major leaguers ask me if they can practice here," said Ueno, who served as Sadahara Oh's translator on the Japanese legend's recent Dominican visit. "I've had [the Expos'] Jose Offerman, Wilton Veras, Jose Mercedes, Josias Manzanillo [of the Cincinnati Reds] all come practice here. I welcome them, because then our players see how to act and how major-leaguers go about their business."

Courtesy of Cody Monk

The Carp's goats finally find the feeding corrals.

Up to 30 players report to the academy each March to begin preparing for the summer season. Players are between 17 and 23 years old, but someone older than 21 is a rarity. Players can play three years in the summer league before they either have to be promoted or released. Since most players sign at 17, a player in his 20s knows he needs to impress quickly.

The Carp quickly get the players into a routine. Living in a 40-person dormitory, players are eating breakfast by 8:30 a.m. Practice runs from 9–12:30, when there is a break for lunch. In the afternoon, there is an additional two-hour practice. Players then go to Japanese language class and then to a practice where nothing but fundamentals are stressed. Dinner is at 7 p.m., followed by free

Carp director Mitsunori Ueno in front of the team's Dominican Summer League trophy.

time in the game room until lights out at 11 p.m. The routine changes only briefly during the season. On game days, afternoon practice is simply moved to before the game. While getting ready for the season, players can go home every 15 days. Once the season starts, the visits are cut to once per month.

"These players have to learn that baseball is their job," Ueno said. "They must concentrate on only baseball. That's the way it is during the season. You have to make an effort in order to have stability. That's why getting them into the routine is so important."

This is the life that awaited Alfonso Soriano. Like the major-league teams, the Carp didn't like how skinny he was or that he was slow. But Ueno said he loved the way the ball jumped off his bat.

"The first time we saw Soriano, he wasn't quite 17 years old. He was far from being developed. But I remember he would put out extraordinary effort, and that is what I really liked," Ueno said. "Also, his moment of impact was so much different than what I had seen before. He had all this power in his wrists. Sometimes you'll see a player have a pause in his swing and then try to generate power. Soriano can do that because not only is he right on top of the ball, but he can pause and then have all that power because of how strong his wrists are."

After conferring with Caesar Geronimo, one of the Carp's two full-time scouts, the Carp offered Soriano approximately $2,000. While it was an offer to play baseball professionally, Soriano didn't knock anyone over looking for a pen.

His mother wanted him to wait to see if any he received any other offers. Andrea's brother, Hilario, reminded her that the Marlins were not likely to offer Alfonso a deal. And he told his sister that if no other major-league teams were in the picture, this would likely be his best opportunity. Jesus Alou also confirmed that there probably weren't going to be any major-league offers. Alfonso wanted to sign, but he and his uncle were going to have to work to convince his mother that it was the right move.

"I didn't want him to sign with the Carp," Andrea said. "I wanted him to wait. I kept telling him, 'Just wait 15 or 20 more days. See what comes in.' He told me 'Mami, I don't want to wait. I want to play ball. I want to buy you a house. I want my mom to live well.' I told him there would be time for all that and he should wait."

Alfonso didn't wait. He signed and was part of the March 1995 crop. He played in the Dominican Summer League, but most of his education took place away from the field. Soriano was learning, along with every other player, that while the game may be the same between the lines, things surrounding the game were very different than what he was accustomed to.

First there was the language barrier. The Carp academy teaches a rigorous Japanese course that gives the players the basics. However, Ueno said it is hard for a lot of the players to learn how to speak a foreign language properly when "they don't even speak correct Spanish." Soriano was one of the rare players who picked up the language fairly easily. His biggest adjustment was the steady diet of fish and fruit, a significant departure from what he had been consuming.

Like any other academy in the Dominican, the Carp took on its share of players who had never eaten a balanced diet. While Soriano, again, was the exception, being on such a rigorous and mandated meal and work schedule took some getting used to. So did the idea of playing fully within the constraints of the Japanese's team concept.

"I remember when we signed Timo [Perez] when he was playing in Japan. He was having a really hard time fitting into their system," said Montreal Expos general manager Omar Minaya, who was then the New York Mets' assistant general manager. "I have a lot of respect and admiration for the Japanese system, but they are focused primarily on the fundamentals. And they want their players to fit into a regimented system."

In the Dominican, players grow up in a system far from regimented. The Dominican system stresses being better than anyone else on the field, teammate or not. Dominican players get their first break because they stand out. Prospects look for that one play a scout can't forget. In the Japanese style, players are expected to be fundamentally sound and make any sacrifice the team needs. If that means that the 30-home run guy needs to lay down a bunt to move a runner along, the 30-home run guy squares around. The two systems would seem to mix about as well as oil and water, but Soriano, happy just to have found a team, was willing to do anything his new employer wanted. But breaking habits that were years in the making wasn't always easy.

"You wouldn't believe how hard I was on Soriano," Ueno said. "I used to make him do laps from foul line to foul line, and I would stand in the middle of the field looking at my watch letting him know he needed to get going. You don't learn baseball with a book. You learn baseball with your body. These players here have to realize that. Soriano did. I got on him a lot here, but I know he appreciated it. He's told me before that it helped make him into a man."

Just after his 18th birthday, the team decided Soriano, who played shortstop and second and third base at the academy, was ready for Japan. Each Japanese team is allowed one minor-league team that plays an 80-game season. Soriano was to play for the Carp's farm team in the Western League, but he would go to full spring training. In the preseason, much like in the major leagues, the Japanese minor leaguers are mixed in with the big club's regulars. The biggest difference between the two spring trainings is the weather. While major-league clubs train in the sun and warmth in Arizona and Florida, the Japanese begin preseason drills in the dead of the Japanese winter.

"One of the biggest differences for Soriano and for Latin players in general in Japan is that perhaps they don't adapt well to the winter training," Ueno said. "I really think that's the case. Japan is a pretty small island,

OPPOSITE: Alfonso forces the Tigers' Shane Halter at second.

"You wouldn't believe how hard I was on Soriano. I used to make him do laps from foul line to foul line, and I would stand in the middle of the field looking at my watch letting him know he needed to get going. You don't learn baseball with a book. You learn baseball with your body. These players here have to realize that. Soriano did. I got on him a lot here, but I know he appreciated it. He's told me before that it helped make him into a man."

**—Carp director
Mitsunori Ueno**

and when it's cold in one place, it's going to be cold all over the country. There isn't a place like Florida where you can go train in the sun. Our training camps are like having training camp in Washington, D.C."

Packing every piece of warm clothing he had into a duffel bag, Soriano headed to Las Americas airport in Santo Domingo on February 8, 1996, for the almost 20-hour trip to Hiroshima.

He survived the brutal weather and the extensive training, but even the language classes and food at the academy hadn't prepared him for this level of culture shock. Perez, who played in front of Soriano in Japan and who had also attended the Carp academy in San Pedro de Macoris, said players always have a hard time adjusting to that first Japanese spring training. However, having few people to talk with and being isolated from the rest of the island takes time to adjust to.

"They give you good training at the academy, but when you get there and you're living in those surroundings and eating the different kind of food and having to talk the different language and having to do it all so quickly, it becomes difficult," said Perez, who played five years in Japan. "The biggest mistake they made with Soriano was when they sent him over they didn't really have anyone to help him who had been there that

spoke his language. They had other Latin players at the time, but there was a lack of people who spoke the language, and there was hardly anyone who had much experience in Japan. Alfonso and I talked a lot during those days."

"Hiroshima can be a hard place, because it's in the southern part of the country. It's in a rural part and is pretty isolated," said Tokahira Nomura, a writer for Tokyo's *Mainichi Shimbun* newspaper. "It's kind of like a football player that is not real comfortable with rural areas going to play in Green Bay."

Because the club was planning to send more Dominicans across the pond, the Carp hired Manny Castillo, who played three years in the big leagues for Kansas City and Seattle, and sent him to Hiroshima to help the team's new charges. Castillo's addition gave Soriano another friend, but it didn't help his performance.

Wearing No. 74, Soriano got his first professional hit on April 21, 1996, against Hanshin's minor-league team. He played in 17 games, hitting .214 with 13 RBIs in 131 at-bats. His only extra-base hits were his five doubles. He stole four bases, walked seven times and had 17 strikeouts.

"When he got to the minor leagues, it was hard on him because of the language and all the changes," Ueno said. "He didn't understand anything that was said. He had

AP/WWP

Alfonso is congratulated by former teammate Gerald Williams.

to have everything translated for him. It was a turning point, though. Right then was the beginning of Soriano's true development."

When he returned to the Dominican for the winter, the club assured him he was very much in their plans. They wanted him to play another year in the minors and possibly move up to the major-league team later in the year. Soriano's mother, Andrea, however, was still not convinced Japan had been the right move.

"When he came back home after that first year in Japan, I could tell he was tired and a little worn out," Andrea said. "I wasn't sure how I felt about him going back. But I told him he had to keep trying. This was his job. He was a baseball player, and he needed to keep getting better. I didn't know about everything that was going on. I had a lot of faith in God. But I do think that everything in Japan was a good experience for him."

In 1997, still in the minors, he got a better opportunity than the previous year. He played in 68 games, raising his average to .252. He had eight home runs, knocked in 34 runs and stole 14 bases. Late in the season, he finally got his chance. On September 26, the Carp brought him up to the big club. He was playing second base but had also played third and shortstop.

"He was fast and had a strong arm," Hiroshima coach Ryuzo Yamazaki said. "Besides that, he had some pop. He was pretty raw, but he had a big upside."

The team used him sparingly the first month. He played in spots before getting his first start against Chunichi on October 24 at the Nagoya Dome. He went 0-2 with a strikeout. In only nine games with the major-league team, Soriano hit .118, getting only two hits in 17 at-bats.

Despite the slow start, Soriano's name was starting to make the rounds among baseball's in-the-know people. He slowly started putting weight on his 132-pound frame. As he got stronger, his speed improved. He still had a cannon hanging from his right arm, and the Carp still marveled at the way the ball flew off his bat.

"Our team still thought a lot of Soriano despite his struggles when he got to the big leagues," Ueno said. "He didn't bat like we knew he could bat, but we still thought he had a bright future with us."

While the on-field personnel wanted to keep what they thought was a 20-year-old star in the making, things started happening off the field after the 1997 season that led to Soriano never playing another game in a Carp uniform. After the season, Soriano's agent, Don Nomura, wanted Soriano's $40,000 salary to be closer to the $220,000 other foreigners in the minor leagues were making. Nomura asked the club for $180,000 a year. The Carp, like most Japanese teams, despised players making a fuss about their contracts. The players were expected to practice hard and play the games, in that order. In March 1998, Nomura, who already had a history of challenging Japanese-league ways—he helped Hideo Nomo get out of his Japanese contract and to the Los Angeles Dodgers—asked the league to serve as an arbiter in the dispute. The commissioner said he would rule in the case, but told Nomura he couldn't be present. Yankees assistant general manager Jean Afterman, then serving as general counsel for Nomura's agency, scrambled to get Soriano ready for the hearing. Despite their efforts, many believed it was a lost cause.

"The Japanese system can be really feudal," said author Robert Whiting, who has written several books on Japanese baseball. "Owners regularly [go against] players, and the players' union is too timid to do anything about it. The commissioner [is beholden] to the owners. It would have been a big surprise if he had decided against them and for Soriano."

The commissioner's proposal wasn't even a meet-in-the-middle offer. On April 13, the league ruled in favor of the club, mandating that Soriano return for $45,000. The experience soured Soriano on going back, and he began focusing on playing in the United States. Soriano and Nomura decided that Nomura would free Soriano much like he did Nomo three years earlier. To become a free agent, Nomo retired from Japanese baseball, meaning he could never return to the Japanese leagues, something normally considered unthinkable during a pitcher's prime years.

A week after losing his arbitration hearing, Soriano also retired. The Carp reacted with a $100,000 defamation lawsuit against Nomura and demanded an apology letter. The team also sent letters to every major-league team threatening legal action if any team signed Soriano.

The suit eventually settled out of court, but the ramifications had only begun to be felt. The decision led to an eventual change in Major League Baseball's agreement with the Japanese leagues where teams now "post" players to the highest bidder. Under the new system, the Japanese club receives at least some monetary compensation for losing a player.

When Soriano retired from the Japanese leagues, Major League Baseball considered him a free agent, because the league assumed he was doing the same thing Nomo had done. When the league received the letter from the Japanese league alerting them of the lawsuit, any possibility of Soriano signing in the States was put on hold. Major League Baseball decided to investigate before deciding what to do.

"We were rattling sabers like crazy," Afterman told the New York *Daily News*. "[We were saying], 'We'll sue MLB if they don't help.'"

The league eventually did help, declaring Soriano a free agent on July 13. At the time, Soriano was in Los Angeles trying to play as much as he could against anyone he could. The competition was a collection of weekend warriors and players who perhaps had some semipro or college experience. Even though he was playing, Soriano didn't feel like he was staying in the kind of shape needed to elicit major-league opportunities. He was also wondering if he had made the right decision to try to play in the States instead of remaining in a situation that had, at least, become familiar.

"Alfonso knew he had the opportunity to play here if he just had the opportunity to do his thing," said Roberto Clemente, Jr. "That time was tough on Alfonso. There were times when he got to a state of depression. He was wondering if he was doing the right thing. A lot of times he was in a daze, but he just kept going because—and this is the one thing about Alfonso above all—he just wanted to play ball."

While Soriano was worrying, major-league clubs were buying stamps in bulk to send letters to the league inquiring about Soriano's status. When clubs were told he was free, Nomura arranged a tryout with eight clubs. The Yankees, Diamondbacks, Brewers, Indians, Cubs, Rockies, Dodgers and Mets all wanted to see if the kid with the .118 Japanese batting average was worth their time.

On the July day Soriano tried out for the Indians, Santana said he was given 17 balls. After blasting one into the parking lot, Omar Vizquel and Sandy Alomar Jr. walked to the cage to see who was doing the blasting. When they were told it was a Dominican kid fresh from the Japanese leagues, Vizquel and Alomar wondered why the Indians weren't shoving a contract in Soriano's face.

"Vizquel and Alomar told Alfonso that day that they wanted him to sign with the Indians," Santana said.

"Alomar said that if he signed with them he would turn into a little Roberto [Alomar]."

What Soriano was doing in the cage was only part of the attraction.

"Players like Soriano have what are called 'electric bodies,'" ESPN analyst and former major leaguer Dave Campbell said. "Everything he does is quick. That's a gift. That's not taught."

Said *ESPN The Magazine* writer Tim Kurkjian: "The thing that makes baseball the greatest sport in the world is that baseball is littered with guys that when you look at their numbers, those numbers aren't exiting. Yet the scouts and people who really know can see a player and say, 'That's a guy who can swing the bat for you.'"

The Indians were so convinced that Soriano could swing the bat for them they offered Soriano a major-league contract on the spot, the first time the club had ever done that after a tryout. The Yankees were so convinced Soriano could hit in their lineup that they offered Soriano a four-year, $3.1 million contract, more than double what any other club was offering.

Soriano signed September 29, 1998, 11 months after playing his last professional game in Japan. With one signature, Soriano's strange journey to the major leagues was about to take yet another turn. He was finally

Seattle Mariners pitcher Jamie Moyer watches as Alfonso trots home after a home run.

going to the United States after his little side trip to Japan. He had just gotten a more than 1,500 percent raise with the majors' most visible team. And the Yankees were considering their find a steal.

Soriano and the Carp both say there are no hard feelings for the way things turned out in Japan. Soriano was free to pursue his big-league dream, and Ueno and the Carp, even though they received no compensation for losing him, were left with the credit for discovering the Yankees' second baseman of the future.

"Alfonso learned so much in Japan," his mother Andrea said. "He learned that baseball was his job, and he learned how to make it

AP/WWP

his job. They gave him an opportunity, and I thank God for that."

Said Ueno: "I think of Soriano like he was my son. His mom still calls, and I still visit her, because I think so much of Soriano as a person. I'll always help them in whatever way I can. I'll advise them in any situation, baseball or not, that they want my help with. Everyone dreams of getting to the big leagues, enjoying the fame, the money. Soriano had that same dream, but he'd still be playing in Japan if he hadn't had the contract problems. Now, he wouldn't be making the same kind of money. But baseball is a business. We all understand that. I respect Alfonso a lot, and I think he respects me. He believes the Japanese experience turned him into a man. We have a great relationship, and I believe we always will. We didn't get anything in return for him, but we will always be able to say we were the ones that found him."

From left, Alfonso, Derek Jeter, and Jason Giambi await their turns in the cage.

4

From Yakyuu to the Yankees

Trey Hillman made sure Alfonso Soriano saw him. The Columbus Clippers' manager didn't move from his place in the dugout, but the look on Hillman's face as Soriano strolled back to the dugout told that young infielder all he needed to know—Hillman was not happy. Soriano knew that later on he would get to hear Hillman's outdoor voice indoors.

Less than a year after signing with the organization, Soriano had shot up the Yankees' food chain. In 1999 alone, Soriano made stops in the rookie league in Tampa, AA Norwich, AAA Columbus and even played nine games with the Yankees. Now early in the 2000 season, the 22-year-old had made an impact that even the highest of Yankees' higher-ups had noticed. But it was Soriano's current supervisor who was about to make an impact on him.

Soriano hit a weak infield grounder that was a sure out. Soriano was so sure he was going to be out that he made a half-hearted attempt at getting to first base. Hillman glared at his young shortstop/second baseman as he slunk down the dugout steps. However, Hillman decided not to teach Soriano a verbal lesson.

OPPOSITE: On his way to big-league stardom, Alfonso made many stops, including a stint with the AA Norwich Navigators.

Courtesy of the Norwich Navigators

"Alfonso loves to play so much that the only way you can ever punish him is to take that away from him," Hillman said.

Hillman immediately took Soriano out of the game. When Soriano came to the park the next day and headed for the infield, someone alerted him to the lineup card. Soriano's name was not on it. It wasn't on there the next day, either.

"He was really upset with me," said Hillman, now the manager of the Nippon Ham Fighters in the Japanese Pacific League. "But I explained to him that we can't forget to run a ball out in this organization. I didn't want him to be allowed to do that."

The benching was almost as tough on Hillman, who describes Soriano as "one of my all-time favorite persons." Hillman knew Soriano was headed for the Bronx soon, but his job was to use, as Hillman said, "tough love" to make the jewel shine.

Hillman spent more time on Soriano's development than any other coach or manager in the Yankees' organization. After he signed in September 1998, Soriano was immediately sent to the Arizona Fall League to play the '98 Fall League season with the Grand Canyon Rafters. Hillman was a Grand Canyon coach for a team managed by Gerald Perry, the former Atlanta Braves and St. Louis Cardinals first baseman and current Pittsburgh Pirates hitting coach. The league, which is sponsored by the major leagues and has six teams, is where organizations send top prospects, mostly their best from AA, for extended seasoning. Players from several teams are on the same team, providing the foundation for lasting friendships among players.

The Rafters finished first in the American Division, going a league-best 26-18 in the 44-game schedule. Pitcher Jason Johnson, now with the Baltimore Orioles, set a league record with seven wins on a team that featured current major leaguers Kerry Robinson (St. Louis) and Chris Singleton (Oakland) in the outfield, pitchers Gabe Molina (St. Louis) and Roy Halladay (Toronto) and infielders Steve Cox (Tampa Bay), Jerry Hairston Jr (Baltimore), Brent Abernathy (Tampa Bay) and Shea Hillenbrand of Arizona.

Soriano wasted little time making an impact on his teammates. Now the Diamondbacks third baseman, Hillenbrand said he was immediately surprised at how much power Soriano had despite being "wiry." With the two, who used to talk before Red Sox–Yankees games, breaking into the majors at the same time, Hillenbrand said he has kept up with Soriano not only because they were rivals, but also because he said he is still amazed at the power and numbers Soriano puts up.

"I remember this guy with just raw power and, bottom line, ability to swing the bat," Hillenbrand said. "With Alfonso, it's all about his bat speed and those quick hands. He also generates so much power from his

Courtesy of the Norwich Navigators

Soriano's personality was quiet, almost introverted at first, but as Soriano got more comfortable in his surroundings, he opened up more in the clubhouse and produced more. The more he produced, the more eyebrows he raised. Soriano hit .254 and led the team in home runs, RBIs and at-bats and tied for the team lead in doubles. It also appeared he hadn't forgotten the endless Japanese practices, even on game days.

One of Hillman's Rafters responsibilities was to work with hitters in the batting cage. Each day, he would open the cage early for anyone who wanted to take additional swings, normally an hour before the team gathered to stretch. Hillman encouraged the Yankees' prospects, in particular, to take advantage of the time. Every day he opened the cage, Hillman said Soriano was there and ready to take cuts. And more cuts. And more cuts. Hillman eventually had to tell Soriano it was okay to take a day off every few days.

On the days before Hillman wanted him to rest, Soriano would get a warning that he needed to save his swings for that day's game.

legs. He's like [former Red Sox teammate] Manny Ramirez in that way."

The league gave Soriano a chance to play against big-time competition again. He spent the first weeks of the fall schedule feeling his way around a familiar game in an unfamiliar land. Soriano already had experience with that. Hillenbrand said

Soriano's run through the league was already making the Yankees' decision to pay him more than double what anyone else was offering look like a bargain. Hillman said the Yankees' timing on the signing couldn't have been more perfect, with Soriano's skills just beginning to blossom and him getting back to doing what he told his mother would be the way he made sure she lived well.

"He felt like he got a new lease on life. He was happy again," Hillman said. "Alfonso is the kind of person that he'll be happy anywhere he is if he knows he's got a game the next day. Emotionally and physically he had just started coming in to his own. The Yankees' hitting program at the time helped him harness those skills. The Yankees had great timing when they decided to sign him. They had it with Jeter in '96 and a bunch of their other players starring for them now. That's something they've always been great at doing." ·

Soriano spent most of 1999 at AA Norwich (Connecticut), where current Yankees first base coach Lee Mazzilli was his manager. By May, Soriano was leading the league in hitting and already had three hitting streaks of 11 games or more. He played 89 games, hitting 15 home runs and stealing 24 bases. He also made the Eastern League All-Star team, a team that included the Angels' David Eckstein and Pat Burrell of the Phillies.

It was yet another moment on the big stage that helped put Soriano on an even faster track to the big show. The day before the 1999 All-Star Game in Boston's Fenway Park, Soriano was part of a group of World prospects taking on United States prospects in the Futures Game. It was here that American fans and the rest of baseball got their first taste of the prospect ESPN analyst Peter Gammons says "has magic moment written all over him."

In leading the World team to a 7-0 win, Soriano went 2-3 with two home runs and five RBIs and won the game's MVP award.

"I remember thinking after he hit those two home runs in the Futures Game, 'Wow, this guy's going to be a great ballplayer,'" said Expos third baseman and San Pedro de Macoris native Fernando Tatis. "He impressed a lot of people in that game."

One of the players he impressed was then-Red Sox pitcher Tomo Ohka, now of the Montreal Expos. Ohka had seen Soriano play in Japan but had never played against him. Being new to the country and not speaking English, Ohka was feeling what Soriano felt in Japan and was partially feeling in the States. Ohka wasn't sure if Soriano spoke Japanese well enough to communicate, but he approached him anyway. When Soriano responded perfectly, Ohka felt he had made a new friend.

"Alfonso is the kind of
person that he'll be
happy anywhere he is if
he knows he's got a
game the next day."

—Columbus Clippers
manager Trey Hillman

"I had always heard he was a quiet guy," Ohka said through an interpreter. "Part of that is the Japanese way that you're supposed to be quiet because of how serious they are. But when I saw him at the Futures Game he was really nice. I was surprised he could speak Japanese. That was nice for me."

Soriano made such an impression on him that Ohka actually looked forward to Red Sox-Yankees games because he would be able to talk to another player. In 2000 spring training, the Red Sox made the trip to Legends Field in Tampa for a spring game with the Yankees. Gammons said camp had been miserable so far with Jimy Williams and Carl Everett battling back and forth. Then, Gammons said, one moment made camp positive for almost everyone.

"Ohka obviously hadn't said anything all camp. He couldn't really communicate with anyone, so no one had ever seen him show much emotion," Gammons said. "The Red Sox get to Tampa that day, and Ohka runs off the bus and onto the field. He runs up to Soriano and gives him this big hug. Then the two start talking in Japanese. [Soriano's] a real nice guy. He's sensitive to other players' situations, and he's very intelligent. But seeing a guy from the Dominican talking Japanese, that was a pretty wild sight."

•••

There are two ways to make a 10-year-old boy really mad in San Pedro de Macoris. The first is a slow drive past the "Bon" ice cream shop without stopping for a dip or two of mint chocolate chip *helado*. The second, and more likely to draw extreme anger, is to tell a kid he's not playing shortstop today.

Taking the ice cream option is a much better choice. Only one kid is mad at a time. Not getting to play shortstop in a pickup game in San Pedro de Macoris is going to make eight other players sulk.

The city is to shortstops what Detroit is to cars and Hollywood is to stars—but on an even bigger level. In San Pedro de Macoris, playing shortstop is the identity of the city. The list of major-league shortstops reads like a Who's Who list from the '80s and '90s: Mariano Duncan, Tony Fernandez, Julio Franco, Alfredo Griffin, Rafael Ramirez—and those are only the ones who made it to the majors as shortstops. Any player from San Pedro de Macoris who has ever played in the Quisqueya Barrio or in one of the countless other places to play in the city has played shortstop—or at least fought to play there.

When Alfonso Soriano was around, the battles were still intense, but they weren't normally as fierce. Teammates deferred to Soriano because they wanted to win. But

that didn't mean that some weren't hoping for a mistake and an opportunity to slide into his spot. The area's history makes competitors among teammates. It instills a pride that becomes almost stubbornness when players are asked to move to a new position.

Even though he played some second and third at the Carp academy, there is no mistaking that Soriano was bred to be a shortstop. It was his identity—where he wanted to play. Like a lot of Latino players, it was where he was determined to play.

"I went to Columbus one day in 2000 to do a story on him, and he told me, 'I am shortstop. That's where I play,'" said Clemente Jr., then working for MSG Network. "At the time they were talking about moving him to the outfield. He said he wasn't doing that. He told me, 'I know Mr. Jeter is at shortstop and Mr. Knoblauch is at second base, but I want to play shortstop.'"

Jeter had been the Yankees' shortstop since 1996. With a new 10-year contract, he wasn't going anywhere. If Soriano was going to play shortstop in the major leagues, it was going to be with another team. And the list of those lined up to give him that opportunity made the cell phone New York

Alfonso slides in safely while Mariners second baseman Brett Boone takes a tumble.

AP/WWP

general manager Brian Cashman's newest piece of jewelry.

Soriano had been an asked-about commodity since his performance in the Arizona Fall League. The speed-power combination from a middle infielder made other general managers willing to give up major names for Soriano. Every time Cashman called to inquire about a piece the Yankees needed between the end of the '98 Fall League season and the start of the 2001 season, the talks started with Soriano.

"Brian Cashman heard, 'Hey, let's talk about Soriano' as much as he heard 'Hello,'" Michael Kay said.

The Angels offered Jim Edmonds. The Dodgers dangled Gary Sheffield. The Blue Jays wanted Soriano to be included in the package for Roger Clemens. Even the A's made a pitch. When trying to decide whether or not to sign him to a long-term contract in 2000, the Cubs offered Sammy Sosa for Yankees prospects, one of which was Soriano.

Before thinking about Sosa or Gonzalez, the Astros had a deal in place to send Moises Alou to the Yankees for pitcher

Ted Lilly and Soriano. Alou, the nephew of Jesus Alou, the scout who originally advised Soriano, used his veto power to nix the trade at the last minute. The same year, the Tigers' Juan Gonzalez did the same, once again in a deal including Soriano.

Soriano's name was still being thrown around as late as the beginning of the 2001 season. Concerned about Soriano's fielding, the Reds and Yankees discussed a Pokey-Reese-for-Soriano deal.

"I called Cashman one day after about the 10th rumor I had heard involving Soriano, this one involving maybe [Toronto's] David Wells," said *ESPN The Magazine*'s Tim Kurkjian. "He said, 'Look, Tim, we're not trading Soriano.' He didn't say it to shut me up, but he was really tired of hearing it all. He knew what he had, and he was tired of hearing all the preposterous rumors that were floating out there."

Most of the rumors came in 2000 when Soriano was playing with AAA Columbus. Hillman said he heard and read about the rumors just like anyone else. His job was to make sure the rumors didn't affect his 22-year-old infielder. Hillman said the talk was hard on Soriano because Soriano had expressed his desire to play in New York. Hillman and Soriano had a few conversations about the rumors, but Hillman decided not to talk extensively about them, choosing

instead to make light of how popular Soriano had become.

"If there was something in the paper that day about a new rumor, we'd come out to the batting cages and say, 'Hey, did you guys see the paper today? Big boy Soriano was in the paper again today,'" Hillman said. "We wanted to make light of the trade talk situation, because he didn't have any control over it."

Hillman said the club didn't talk much directly to him about trading Soriano. On the one deal the club did decide to consult Hillman on, he made sure the club knew his feelings. Still searching for outfield help in 2000, the Yankees were pursing Montreal's Rondell White. The Expos wanted Soriano in return. Hillman heard the rumors and called "someone in the organization with a lot more juice than Trey Hillman." Hillman told the club that while he understood their situation, he believed that if they traded Soriano at that point they would not only be making a mistake, but that it would be one of the few trades in his baseball career that he "would take personally and get emotional about."

"For the first time in my 13 years with the Yankees, I stepped out of my box a little bit on the Rondell White thing," Hillman said. "It wasn't a question of me not having respect for the job [management] was doing,

OPPOSITE: Alfonso slides into second while Red Sox shortstop Rey Sanchez tries to make the play.

because as I managed up the ladder I got a much better understanding and feel of how much thought, preparation and study went into those decisions. It was a matter of me having an opportunity to be around this kid day in and day out."

The emotion Hillman felt was because he was starting to see Soriano's raw baseball talent develop into refined skills. Hillman was also seeing one of his tougher baseball decisions starting to play out positively.

In 2000, the organization wanted Soriano to play in Columbus and learn to play either second base or in the outfield. He would be competing with D'Angelo Jimenez, a fellow Dominican and another

highly touted Yankees prospect that the club had been reluctant to part with. With both on the roster, Hillman would have to split shortstop time between the two. He knew maintaining a delicate time balance was a must. Even though Soriano and Jimenez were now professionals, both still fought for the shortstop position like they were playing pickup in Santo Domingo's Parque Olímpico. When Soriano played shortstop, Jimenez was at second and vice versa.

Neither liked the arrangement and complained enough to Hillman that the manager had finally had enough. He sat the two down for a lengthy conversation, telling them both that the move was being made

OPPOSITE: Alfonso celebrates a Yankees victory with his teammates.

because the Yankees already had their shortstop of the future. Hillman suggested the quickest way to New York was to make an impression at second and let the Yankees know they did the right thing in not trading them. The talk was a blow to both, especially to their pride.

"I told them that the quicker they put their Latino/Dominican Republic pride of having to play shortstop behind them and start worrying about how they could contribute to the big club, the better off both of them were going to be," Hillman said. "I told them that a very talented young man was playing shortstop in New York that had been there since '96, and that they were competing against each other for status on a AAA team. Neither one of them liked it. It took Soriano a week before he was having fun again because he was so frustrated," Hillman said.

There it was. Soriano had yet another wall in front of him. To get over this one he was going to have to move across the diamond to a position that, while not unfamiliar, was certainly not natural. At shortstop, Soriano displayed the same aggression that he did at the plate. He attacked balls and did, as Peter Gammons said, "everything quick." At second, he would have to harness that aggression and play more under control.

Plenty of players had made the switch from short to second effectively. Chicago White Sox second baseman Roberto Alomar came up as a shortstop, as did the Expos' Jose Offerman, Soriano's San Pedro de Macoris neighbor, and both have made careers playing second base after an initial transition period.

Offerman said the biggest difference is the speed. At short, he said, everything happens in front of you. Because of that, he said, you have to keep everything moving at the same quick pace.

"You wouldn't think there would be a huge difference, but there is," Offerman said after a workout at the Dodgers' Campo Las Palmas facility outside Santo Domingo. "Shortstop is more difficult, because everything comes at you so rapidly. The angles are different at second. That's the biggest thing you have to learn moving over, because you're used to seeing the ball coming at you one way, and now it's bouncing at you differently."

When Roberto Alomar was making his way through the San Diego organization, he was in a similar situation to Soriano's. Gary Templeton was the Padres' shortstop, and Alomar was told that if he wanted a quick ticket to the big leagues, he had to make a position change. Much like Soriano, he didn't take the news well, and, he admits, it was mostly because of pride.

"When you're asked to switch positions, it's normally because the club sees something in you that's going to get you to the big leagues quicker," Alomar said. "That's what happened to me. I was signed as a shortstop, but they already had a guy there that was going to be there a long time. That's the point where you've got to tell a guy it's not about ego. It's about what's going to get you to the big leagues faster."

Soriano made the switch, but the Yankees were concerned it was going to take him a while to make the transition. The team also had a sour taste in its mouth from Soriano's first big-league experience.

The Futures Game performance in 1999 earned Soriano a trip to AAA Columbus and a reunion with Hillman. After 20 games, Hillman got a call that Soriano was needed in New York to fill in for the injured Scott Brosius—at third base. Soriano had played some third in the Japanese leagues, but Hillman almost wanted to close his eyes and not look when he found out where his prized pupil had to play.

Soriano played in nine games. He got his first major-league hit—a home run off Tampa Bay's Norm Charlton—but that would turn out to be his only hit in eight at-bats. He also made four errors. When Brosius returned, Soriano was sent back to Columbus. That is when Hillman picked up the phone.

"I called Willie Randolph and told him he had to work with the guy one-on-one," Hillman said. "[Soriano] went up there and didn't hit much and made some errors. They soured on him, but the poor guy wasn't comfortable. He hadn't had time at third, and he was doing it in the arena of New York City and Yankee Stadium. That's when I called Willie, just to give him some insight into Alfonso's personality. I told Willie that if he'd just work with the kid and let him take some ground balls, he'd be fine."

Though Soriano was going to spend the year at Columbus, Randolph did drill his new pupil when spring training rolled around in 2000. The Yankees gave Soriano a shot at short early in the year when Derek Jeter was hurt. Soriano hit only .180 in 22 games, but his first two hits were home runs, making him the first player since Boston's Mike Greenwell in 1985 to hit home runs in his first three major-league hits. It was back to Columbus when Jeter was healthy, but Soriano did get to experience the 2000 postseason. That year, the Yankees beat the Mets in the World Series, a series that his good friend Timo Perez had played a large role in getting the Mets to and for which Soriano got a ring.

Alfonso Soriano is safe at second with a leadoff first-inning double as the Boston Red Sox' Damian Jackson waits for the throw.

columnist and talk show host. "He gets the newspaper every day and just pours over the box scores. He reads every one. He'll come up with this. Watch."

The ice cream now soft, Billy pipes up loud enough for the nearby tables to hear.

"It's Joe Randa! I knew I knew it," Billy proclaims.

Billy is warm now. Who are Atlanta's starters? He quickly rolls through the Braves' starting rotation. Who do you like better, Pedro Martinez or Randy Johnson? Billy says he takes Randy over Pedro because "a power pitcher who strikes batters out in the National League is more dominating that what Pedro does in the American League." He knows that Tom Glavine is a New York Mets pitcher now because the Braves "left him free."

Eventually Billy, who during the season watches games and then writes game stories that he gives to his dad for corrections and advice, shows he is still a 10-year-old. He says that instead of Miguel Tejada, Alex Rodriguez or Derek Jeter at shortstop, he'd take San Francisco's Neifi Perez. "[Perez] is my friend," Billy points out.

By this time, the nearby table has joined the conversation. Will Tejada sign a long-term deal? How about the year Soriano had? Can he keep it up? Why didn't Sammy Sosa come home this winter?

None of this fazes the Rojas family. It could be in the *Pelequeria Vosso* barber shop, the TGIFriday's in Plaza Acrópolis or the Hooters-like "Eagle" bar in East Santo Domingo, a popular hangout for ballplayers. Everyone not only talks baseball, they talk baseball well. Topics on a normal taxi ride in the capital will range from Pedro's health to how Soriano and his buddy Vladimir Guerrero of the Expos were both one home run short of 40-40 last season.

On the bustling Santo Domingo seafront, waves pound rocks only yards away from cars speeding down George Washington Avenue. The pounding causes a mist every 30 seconds that can be felt on the opposite side of the street. Just down from the swanky, waterfront Hotel Jaragua and V Centenario Hotel is a line of restaurants ready to serve "pinchos de res" by the dozen.

At the Mio Bar, meringue music blasts so loud the waitress has to lean in and yell to take an order. The bar has six wooden tables with four chairs around each that are wooden with the backs woven in rope. There certainly is no set table arrangement. On most nights, the tables and chairs are outside the place, which has no front door. The music leads to impromptu dancing on the George Washington sidewalks. Customers drink Presidentes, the national beer of the Dominican, and can order, among other

OPPOSITE: Balmy breezes blow along the picturesque Santo Domingo beachfront.

things, a Cuban sandwich, Ritz Bits crackers and Zacanitas (Frosted Flakes). The full moon is partially covered by scattered clouds, but enough light shines through for the dancers to feel the cool ocean breeze that makes the palm trees just out of their reach sway from side to side.

Outside the bar, out of the view of Santo, the owner, Richard and his cronies, a group of three 11-year-old shoeshine boys, lie in wait for unsuspecting tourists. They come equipped with old, homemade wooden boxes carrying soap and a rag that likely used to be a T-shirt or a pants leg. They stare long into their prospective customers' eyes and already have their sales pitch down. If you give in to a RD$10 shine (less than $0.50 USD) and throw in an extra RD$10 for the rest of the crew, you've got conversation for hours. These boys play baseball every day. They also know where to find "los prospectos" (the prospects) because, in a few years, these kids will be the prospects. Even though Soriano grew up differently than most Dominican players, these shoeshine boys could be the next Sosa, who, 25 years ago, strolled around San Pedro de Macoris looking for anyone needing a shine.

The Dominican Republic has long been referred to as a baseball-loving nation— a place where baseball is religion. While it is those things, the game—if it is possible—

has an even deeper significance. It is ingrained in the culture because, to those who play, it is often much more than a diversion. Baseball can be the way out of a country where the average annual wage struggles to reach $3,500 USD.

Kids like Richard don't play for college scholarships or to impress girls in their high school class. Many quit school around age 13 to concentrate on baseball. The goal is to show the "buscones" enough that one takes you under his wing and develops you into a player who gets a cherished spot at one of the pristine major-league academies around the country. That means going to school once or twice a week, if that much. Richard promises he goes to English class every day. After some grilling, he recants and admits he makes it every now and then, when he and his family can afford for him to go. It's not the cost that concerns his family. The concern is how much Richard needs to work so his family can have a meal that night.

When Sosa and Mark McGwire of the St. Louis Cardinals were chasing Roger Maris's home run record in 1998, those around Barrio Mexico in San Pedro de Macoris were certain that McGwire would get the record first. Not that there wasn't confidence in the hometown hero. According to Sosa's buddies, McGwire had better living conditions as a child. He had

OPPOSITE: A hopeful fisherman casts his line in the Caribbean waters.

ALFONSO SORIANO

AP/WWP

"better toys" and an easier upbringing because he grew up in the United States. As Sosa's sister, Sonia, told *The Dallas Morning News*, Sosa "ate plantains and rice growing up, not steak" like everyone assumed McGwire did.

Many Dominican players grow up where the daily goal is to find food for that day. In a lot of cases, baseball takes priority over school, because the game can eventually alleviate the necessity of wondering where the next meal is coming from for a number of family members. Among Latin players, *quitando la comida* (taking away food) is a popular phrase to describe when a Latin player beats an American player out for a job.

"When I'm pitching I think of it as: I'm earning my 'comida,'" said Red Sox pitcher Pedro Martinez, who is from Manoguayabo, just off the San Juan River in the western part of the country. "I think of the hitter as someone trying to take food off my mom's and dad's table."

To many players, the game is about much more than wearing the big gold and signing multimillion-dollar contracts. It's about playing well enough that your family doesn't have to struggle. It's about impressing the community where your roots are likely very deep. Most players were born and raised in the same town. People they ran with as kids are the people they still run with, no matter what that friend might do currently. Players are held in high regard in the Dominican, especially among the children. However, among people close to the same age as the player, there is almost no awe. Because, as Rojas said, the Dominican Republic is a country where it "seems like everyone knows everyone, and everyone acts that way." The players' childhood friends remain their closest friends even when the big baseball money and fame rolls in.

"Fame and fortune, for the most part, don't affect us," said Montreal third baseman Fernando Tatis. "Most of us come from the lower class or middle class, and we've all got a lot of common bonds, ballplayers or not. We had our friends growing up, and there's no reason to change when you get here."

Rarely does a big-money contract change a Dominican player. Like Tatis, Martinez, who makes over $14 million per year, said that goes back to the struggles growing up.

"What you have to realize is that even the minimum salary in baseball is a lot of money to us," Martinez said. "We're only here because we made the most of an opportunity that was given us. The money doesn't change who we are."

These deep-rooted ties extend among the Latin baseball community. Whether the player is from the Dominican, Venezuela,

Alfonso is congratulated by the Yankees' Juan Rivera after bashing a two-run homer.

Puerto Rico, Panama or Mexico, there is a sense of responsibility from the older players to make sure the younger players are shown the correct way of doing things. *La cadena* (the chain) makes sure that when a player like Soriano comes up and doesn't understand what is going on culturally or what is being said, he has a veteran player to lean on.

"Soriano is still doing a lot of learning," said Yankees closer Mariano Rivera, one of the players, along with Bernie Williams, who has guided Soriano since his arrival in the Bronx. "There is a responsibility, because when the guy first comes here, he doesn't know. He's your teammate, and in some cases from the same country you are. You feel a responsibility to show him what it has been like being in the major leagues."

In major-league clubhouses, teams normally have a congregation of Latin players. For example, Rivera, Williams and Soriano all have lockers close to one another in Yankee Stadium. The Latin players like to be close simply for language reasons, but also to be around if a younger player has a question about how things are done.

Expos general manager Omar Minaya, the first Latino general manager, has seen *la cadena* work both as a scout and now in management. Minaya, who found Juan Gonzalez and Sammy Sosa for the Texas Rangers, said before last season he specifically signed Venezuelan first baseman Andres Galarraga because Latin players "have that respect and understanding of helping younger players.

"It's about connecting with someone who's accustomed to something you've been accustomed to," Minaya said. "The older [Latin] players like to help the younger players. That's the reason I brought [Galarraga] on board last year, and I'm hoping [Cuba's Orlando Hernandez] is that guy this year."

"The best way to learn is by example," said White Sox second baseman Roberto Alomar. "The young guys need to communicate with the veteran guys. I think you learn more by watching. That's what I did coming up. I had a lot of players talking to me, helping me. Now it's my turn."

•••

Santo Domingo's Parque Olímpico is not hard to find. The park sits on the corner of Avenida Máximo Gomez and 27th de Febrero. (February 27 is the Dominican Independence Day, and most Latin American countries have streets named after their version of July 4th.) There is a giant billboard of Pedro Martinez asking kids to stay off drugs that welcomes visitors. The park has volleyball and basketball courts and plenty of room for spreading out or working out. These places have their regulars, but the main attractions, as anyone on the street can tell you, are the four baseball fields on the north side of the park.

The *campos de beisbol* (baseball fields) are vacant lots with fences around them. Grass is spotty, and the fields are so worn that even the slowest of rollers is a potential broken nose. Runners slide at their own risk. On a lazy Sunday afternoon, two of the pickup fields are packed while the third field has three players hitting grounders to each other at third base.

The first field is for the players who do play the game for fun. Most were never true prospects. They work in the bank building across the street; some work in the hotels on the *Malecón* (seafront drive); some drive cabs. They come from all walks of life, bonded by baseball.

The real action is on the park's farthest north field. Here, a group of 13- to 19-year-olds have gathered in a barrio vs. barrio game, which does feature several prospects. The field is very much the obstacle course the other fields are, but few of the players have problems. Most of them play here so much that they know the surroundings better than their own homes.

The bases are old boxes weighted down by both nails and rocks. Players have normal bats and balls—most provided by local major- and minor-league players when they return in the winter from playing overseas. The catchers have a full set of equipment, even though it's shared between the teams. There is one batting helmet that gets tossed to home plate from wherever the runner ends up. When a ball goes sailing over the 320-foot sign in left field, the left fielder has to climb the wall and retrieve one of only two available balls.

It's late February. The Dominican Winter League season has just ended. The Dominican Republic has just won the Caribbean Series with a team stocked with Oakland's Miguel Tejada, Raul Mondesi of the Diamondbacks, Baltimore's Tony Batista and Boston's David Ortiz, who was the MVP of the Series. Spring training is in full swing, but these players at Parque Olímpico aren't really thinking about that right now. They are battling each other—battling to stand out.

They are battling over a close safe call at home plate after a wild pitch that sends both teams running to the field and the umpire—a 16-year-old kid who happened not to be playing that day—running toward the nearest exit. The pitcher who tossed the wild pitch is pulled the next inning. He isn't so much upset about being taken out of the game as he is about having to give the ball *and* his glove to the reliever. In classic Latino style, the second baseman and shortstop are always moving around when a runner is at second—that "one-handed, flashy aggression," that Yankees third base coach Willie Randolph said is so common to Latin shortstops.

When a runner decides on his own to score from first on a double, only to be thrown out by at least three feet, a major argument ensues. The argument spills over to the five older men standing at the bottom of the bleachers to the right of home plate. None can believe the kid would try to score on that. Others point out how ill-advised the catcher's throw to first was after making the tag on the runner. Even the littlest fans have an opinion. Between the men's screams,

AP/WWP

Teammates Alfonso and
outfielder Raul Mondesi.

AP/WWP

an eight-year-old yells to no one in particular: "The throw was bad! The throw was bad!"

The shouts are barely heard because of the noise going on in the stands. A group of four 10-year-old boys are beating an old washboard with branches they found on the ground next to the trees behind the stands. When the bandleader isn't looking, a mischievous little girl steals the drum and the chase is on. Ten minutes later, the bandleader returns, but he does not have his drum. Instead, he finds an old milk crate top and starts beating that in support of his team. The leader eventually loses one of his buddies, who decided to question a newcomer. The 10-year-old tells his mates that the outsider is *un scout*. The outsider says he's just there to enjoy the game, but the kid isn't buying. He sees the writing, the watching and more writing. This guy definitely has to be someone looking for a prospect.

Even those as young as this boy understand how the system works. You play your guts out on fields like Parque Olímpico in hopes that there is a scout standing around who wants to show you off. The players never know when and where a scout will show up.

One Tuesday morning in February, a game is already in the sixth inning when the third basemen points out two men he knows.

The third baseman is Luis Alou, son of San Francisco Giants manager Felipe Alou. He points out to his teammates that the two men standing next to each other behind the south dugout are scouts. One is Pablo Neftali Cruz, a former Pittsburgh Pirates scout who signed Tony Peña, Aramis Ramirez and Abraham Nuñez, among others. The other is a scout known simply as "Papiro."

In the Dominican, everyone has a nickname. Most stick so well that even people who have known the person for years have no idea what the person's real name is. Papiro used to live in New York and now runs a school in Santo Domingo prepping players for tryouts. Papiro and Cruz get paid to find players. Today there is talk about "a switch-hitting Alex Rodriguez out in San Cristobal." Tomorrow it will be another hot prospect everyone just has to see. When one of these "must-see" players advances through an organization, the buscones are justly rewarded.

The players not lucky enough to be a can't-miss prospect whom the scouts drool over compete for attention with teammates and opposition on fields like this every day. The goal is to get one of these scouts to think enough of you to take you to a much-treasured "tryout day" at one of the academies.

Alfonso and shortstop Derek Jeter.

Major-league teams have scouted and mined Dominican talent for decades. No team has been as successful as the Los Angeles Dodgers and their Campo Las Palmas academy outside Santo Domingo. The road leading to the academy runs through the east side of town and through the Dominican Republic's version of the United States Military Academy at West Point. Each side of the highway is covered in thick vegetation with sugarcane almost pouring over into the road. Makeshift buildings with tin roofs that look like storage buildings for the sugarcane harvesting equipment are actually field workers' homes. Suddenly, cut out of the cane fields and palm trees is a patch of green fields and outfield walls. The complex has four fields and two complete stadiums with major-league dimensions, including a 400-foot center field.

About 10–15 Class A players are taking batting practice, waiting for the word on where in the U.S. they will be playing this year. The best of this bunch are at the

American consulate awaiting final word on their visas. One player stands out among the crowd of mixed and matched hats and jerseys. He is wearing a black T-shirt and hitting balls harder than any other player, even though he is mixing with them like he was just another minor-league prospect headed to the rookie league.

"That's Jose Offerman," complex supervisor Eleodoro Arias says of the 13-year major-league veteran, adding that Raul Mondesi, who won the 1994 National League Rookie of the Year while playing for the Dodgers, and Pedro Martinez's brother Ramon, also a Dodgers signee, also return when they can. "A while back I had Pedro and [Pedro] Astacio [both of whom were Dodgers signees] come back to give a talk to the kids. We want the kids to see how big leaguers act."

Campo Las Palmas set the standard for Dominican academies. It has the Tom Lasorda Dining Room, a weight and training room and dorms for up to 110 players. Players are up by 6:45 and don't stop for lunch until 12:45. Brief English classes are followed by weight room sessions and then watching baseball on TV or quiet time.

The biggest difference for the players are the three balanced, daily meals. Many signed players have never eaten on a regular schedule and are so skinny that they are considered malnourished. Because many have little or no education, the academy often has to teach the players from scratch.

"The academies have to do things as basic as teach the kid how to hold a fork," Rojas said. "It's like starting all over and teaching a 17-year-old toddler."

Even though 17 is the age players can actually sign, players prepare for that day much earlier. As the sun was going down one day in Santo Domingo's Parque Mirador del Sur, a father was pitching acorns to his six-year-old boy, who was hitting the nuts with a four-foot-long piece of PVC pipe. The father explains they are playing *Vistilla*, a game where something so small is pitched that the batter has to strain his eyes just to see it. The game is normally played with the cap from the bottom of an industrial-sized water cooler. The father begins to explain that it is important to get scouts looking way before age 17. After 17, he explains, the chances of a contract are slim, because the scouts want someone younger that they can develop while the player is still growing.

"You hear debates on both sides of the so-called magical age 17," Rojas said. "But there is no mistake that it is very important. Not just because that's when they can sign, but because it can signal whether a player is going to be signed or be one of the ones cast aside."

Those who don't get signed end up on the field on Parque Olímpico's south side playing for fun—some with jobs, some barely surviving. Those who do sign still come back. They talk and play and talk and play some more. Just like they've always done—only in nicer clothes. While watching pickup games, a tall, slender 20-year-old dressed in nice jeans, a Tommy Hilfiger shirt and a New York Mets baseball cap walks over to the two guys selling freshly squeezed orange juice. The man in front buys two glasses and offers one to the Mets prospect standing behind him.

"During the [major league] off season," said Rojas, "you're just as likely to see Pedro Martinez or Sammy Sosa down here as you are any other person. It's just not that big of a deal. The kids look up to them, but it's nothing for them to be standing around like anyone else."

It is yet another example of the players feeling a need to give back. Many players bring back every pair of cleats, hats, gloves, socks, pants—whatever the major-league team can spare. Because of the number of players who bring stuff back, a young prospect often is wearing a mix of major-league team gear. On this Tuesday afternoon, the pitcher is wearing an Expos hat, but eats his hot dog between innings with a Cincinnati Reds jacket draped over his pitching arm.

"The best way to describe it is that everyone loves baseball," said Arizona outfielder Raul Mondesi. "Kids will play in the streets, on any kind of field. They do it 24 hours a day. But the people are a very humble kind of people. And even though there's a lot of playing and competition, it's really laid back."

Players' ties to their towns and friends breed competition. While American fans and players may think the winter leagues are where players not quite ready for the majors go for more seasoning, Latin players see it a different way. The roots in these places dictate that they play winter ball. This is a chance for it to be like it was when they were kids, when the major-leaguers of today were kids scrambling for a spot in a pickup game. There is an obligation culturally and, to most Latin players, an internal desire to play.

This past winter, Soriano was set to play with his team, the Estrellas Orientales, until the Yankees expressed concern about him playing winter ball. He thought he had the go-ahead to play the last game of the season and the 18-game round-robin playoff. In his uniform and ready to play, Soriano got word that he wasn't cleared to play. He had to sit on the sidelines and watch.

"If you don't live it, you don't understand it," said Roberto Clemente Jr., whose father is an icon for Latin players.

"Alfonso is still learning, but, I tell you, his joy is contagious."

—Yankees center fielder Bernie Williams

Alfonso and Texas Rangers shortstop Alex Rodriguez clown around before the 2002 All-Star game in Milwaukee.

AP/WWP

"That's your island. That's your land. When you're a kid you watch all the ballplayers come back and play for the local teams, and so that's what you want to do. To be able to be seen in the hometown uniform, that's pride. The money, hurting the major-league team or getting hurt is not something you think about. You play because you have a passion to play."

"Not playing was really hard on Alfonso," said Santana. "He would go to the games and watch, and that was just as hard on him as if he had been there playing, because he was cheering and getting so into the games."

•••

As a 12-year veteran, Yankees center fielder Bernie Williams has earned the right to poke a little fun at Alfonso Soriano.

"Alfonso is still learning, but, I tell you, his joy is contagious," Williams said. "Alfonso is always willing to try, which means he's going to fail sometimes, but it also means he's going to learn. He loves to say things in Spanish that make perfect sense in Spanish but when he tries to translate to English, they don't really translate. In batting practice he'll tell the pitcher it's 3-0 and then say something like *¿Ahora que?* [Now what?] It translates okay to English, but in Spanish it makes much more sense. His English is not as good as he wants it to be, but he's not afraid to speak it."

As great as his 2002 season was and as great as future seasons might be, right now Soriano is just another link in *la cadena*. He is still learning the game, the culture and the ins and outs of being a major leaguer. As his career continues and improves, he will still be just another link. Even when he retires he'll still be a link. It's the way of a Latin player. The chain keeps going. The older ones teach the younger ones.

"It's our responsibility to help the younger guys," Tatis said. "When I first came up [in the Rangers organization], guys like Juan [Gonzalez] and Pudge [Rodriguez] helped me. That was something that made an impression on me. I have to pass that on. That's my responsibility."

Soriano will quickly be one of the players giving advice. With Soriano still keeping up with his Japanese skills, he already is the one Yankees player who can communicate with new right fielder Hideki Matsui. And his English is getting better. Soriano watches American movies on DVD so he can rewind parts and make sure he's got the phrases down. He is now comfortable doing interviews in the language, showing yet another area where he is a quick learner.

"After the [2001] World Series year, Susan Waltman, who was working for WFAN at the time, wanted to interview him," Yankees television broadcaster Michael Kay said. "He didn't want to, because he didn't feel comfortable with his English. She told him, 'Let's get this straight. When you come to spring training [in 2002] you're going to be able to speak English well enough to do an interview with me, okay?' He made it a point to make himself speak it. He was dead set on improving his communication with the media. That showed me a lot about him that he wanted to learn to converse with teammates and the media."

Once again, *la cadena* works. With a locker close to Williams and Rivera, both of whom speak English very well, Soriano watched, listened and learned to how to communicate with those who tell your story.

"Talking with the media is part of your job as a baseball player," Rivera said. "I haven't taken any classes, but I learned by talking to my teammates and having them teach me things. I've told Alfonso this. I told them I'm going to try, and I don't care if they laugh at me for saying something wrong. They can laugh all they want, as long as they'll correct me and teach me."

On the field, there appears to be little left for Soriano to learn. His 2002 season will rank as one of the most productive ever for a middle infielder. He does need to improve on his 157 strikeouts, which broke Danny Tartabull's club record. Scouts say that much like Sammy Sosa, Soriano will improve his walk numbers.

Sosa didn't have more than 58 walks in a season until his ninth season, the year he hit 66 home runs (1998). Sosa has also had four seasons where he has struck out more than 165 times. In 2002, Soriano walked only 23 times, which was six fewer than the previous year.

"He's so aggressive that even if he misses he's going to give you a good pass," Williams said. "Really, there's no good way to pitch him. You can keep nibbling, but at some point you've got to throw something over the middle of the plate."

Said Yankees pitcher Andy Pettite: "He's really good at jumping on the first pitch. But if you start him off with a first-pitch slider and then try to throw all off-speed stuff, you can see him almost start coaxing the pitcher into a mistake. He's tough to pitch to, because he can hit balls out of the strike zone. He's a really good bad-ball hitter."

So what does Soriano do for an encore? White Sox second baseman Roberto Alomar warned about expecting this kind of season every year. Alomar said that Soriano could reach 30-30 and people might consider it "a down year."

"Barring injury, he'll have another tremendous year," ESPN analyst Dave Campbell said.

In San Pedro de Macoris, Yankees games have always been a draw because of the logo

and because the Yankees television network (YES) reaches the Dominican Republic. That's fine with Andrea Soriano, who prefers to watch her son's games on television. When she does go to New York, as she did last summer when she lived with him for a month between the middle of July to the middle of August, she'll cook for him and stay on top of him about the things she always does.

"I always want him to keep a smile on his face," Andrea said. "Growing up, I always smiled, and I always told Alfonso, 'You don't want to ever have an ugly face. You always want to be handsome in all you do.' That's where that big smile comes from."

As far as the pressure of playing in New York and the pressure of getting close, again, to the 40-40 mark (or the 50-50 that first baseman Jason Giambi predicted Soriano could attain), Andrea said those kinds of things have to be put into perspective.

"Alfonso loves to play baseball. That's his job and he loves it. And he loves New York," Mrs. Soriano said. "He doesn't feel pressure. Playing baseball isn't pressure. Pressure is raising four kids in Barrio Quisqueya as a single parent."

However, Andrea does have one request that might put some pressure on her baby.

"I've told Alfonso that before I die I want him to have a year," Andrea said, "where he hits either 75 or 80 home runs."

If it ever happens, San Pedro de Macoris will turn into complete anarchy. Only this time, Mami Soriano will be watching.

him a target for the older Latin players to teach perspective. It also afforded Soriano the opportunity to be a role model to new players coming up. That's the way it works. You start at the bottom and slowly earn the right to move to a higher link on the chain as your baseball skills and your comfort level become more and more seasoned.

The new leadership role didn't affect Soriano on the field. With Jeter out, Soriano snatched the headlines and started sparking Triple Crown talk. He had 16 multi-hit games in April and a career-high 15-game hit streak. Soriano got out of the gates by going 14-31 with three homers the first week of the season. For the rest of the month, there would only be three days in which he didn't get a hit. The April 29 game against Seattle was the only game that first month in which he wasn't on base.

Hall of Fame second baseman Joe Morgan, who won the National League MVP in 1975 and '76 with the Cincinnati Reds, wrote in an ESPN.com story that even in a lineup that features big names like Jason Giambi and Bernie Williams, the wiry second baseman "has become the offensive leader of the Yankees." Morgan wrote that Soriano, through the first six weeks of the season, was, offensively, "head and shoulders" above any other American League hitter. Morgan also predicted that Soriano would be the first second baseman in 44 years to bring home the MVP trophy.

Soriano's magical 2002 started fast, but nothing like 2003. And in 2002, the Yankees had advance warning that something special was about to happen. Soriano stormed through the 2002 spring as the major's standout spring player. Because the Yankees wanted to see how well he could hit leadoff, Soriano had more at-bats than anyone else that spring. He hit, continued to hit and continued to shine. He showed enough that the Yankees stuck him in the opening day lineup, and there he has remained.

Though he wasn't expected to get much of a workload this spring, a recurring shoulder problem had the team worried even before camp opened. Soriano insisted it was nothing, but eyebrows were raised when he pulled out of a February home run-hitting contest in Las Vegas. When the Yanks threw the doors open at Legends Field in Tampa, Soriano was there, throwing, fielding and, of course, hitting. He kept insisting the shoulder was no problem. However, he sat out the spring opener against the Reds and would miss six spring training games.

Part of the missed time had nothing to do with a bum shoulder. It had everything to do with the passing of a man Soriano's mother, Andrea, described as Soriano's "hero" while growing up. Cecilio Guzman, Andrea's father, died March 10 in San Pedro de Macoris. He was 89. He was also the male role model for Alfonso and his two brothers after Andrea got divorced when Alfonso was young.

Because his mother didn't want her children to have a stepfather, Andrea moved back in with her parents and raised Alfonso, his two brothers and sister. Every summer, Guzman donned his old hat, grabbed a stick and headed into the sugar cane fields with his three grandsons in tow, showing them, according to Andrea, "how to work hard." Andrea said Alfonso hated working in the fields ("He looked forward to getting back to school," she said), but that the experience is the reason he is blessed with the work ethic so many in the Yankees organization praise him for having.

Soriano never let on publicly that the passing had an effect on him. Guzman, however, was a central figure in Soriano's childhood. Certainly more than his father, Carlos Gilliard, who died in the Dominican Republic two months later and who hadn't been a part of Alfonso's upbringing since before Alfonso turned seven.

"Alfonso [loved] his grandfather and he certainly thought a lot of Alfonso," Andrea said. "Alfonso works hard at everything he does. That's what his grandfather taught him. Always have respect for other people and everything you do."

While at home for the funeral, Andrea did what she always does with her youngest child. She encouraged him, told him to concentrate on baseball and understand that "God will always be with you. He won't give you anything you can't handle."

It took Soriano a few days to get back, emotionally and physically. The shoulder was still bothering him. He still had 60 spring at-bats, but he hit only .250 with two home runs and four RBIs.

In addition to dealing with his grandfather's death, Soriano was a man, technically, playing without a contract. His original four-year, $3.1 million deal he signed after leaving Japan in 1998 expired before camp. The Yankees and Soriano's then-agent, Don Nomura, talked about a long-term deal, but couldn't come to an agreement. Because he had only two years' major-league service time, Soriano wasn't eligible for salary arbitration or free agency. If he was going to play, the Yankees were going to dictate the terms, to a certain point. The team made it clear they wanted to make Soriano a nice one-year offer. The Yankees offered $800,000 (a $170,000 raise), even though under the MLB collective bargaining agreement New York could have offered him a 20 percent pay cut, and it would be the only contract offer he would get for the season.

He signed in spring training, making the contract the biggest deal ever for the team for a player with two years' experience and who wasn't yet eligible for free agency. The deal gave the Yankees a potential 40-40 player at second base on the cheap. It also allowed Soriano the opportunity to walk into arbitration next season and get himself an

OPPOSITE: Alfonso avoids a sliding Chuck Knoblauch and snags a throw at second base.

even bigger contract. That is, provided he had a year worthy of a raise.

After the first month, it looked like the Yankees would have to simply pay whatever Soriano asked for. He was mashing balls, helping the Yankees build one of the best records in the game and leading a team missing its captain.

Then, as things have a tendency to do in baseball, things began to even out. He went through a 1-19 slump in a five-game swing through the tough arms of AL West stalwarts Seattle and Oakland. And even though he had a seven-game and a six-game hitting streak, he hit only .229 in May, dropping his average from .371 to .302. Soriano was also taking his hitting woes to the field, something Randolph had warned Soriano about since last season.

In the Yankees' April 25 win over Texas, Soriano popped out to end the New York ninth. With two outs in the bottom of the ninth, Carl Everett hit a bouncer behind the mound, a play Soriano normally makes. Instead, the ball went through and Everett reached. Michael Young then hit a ball toward second, something Randolph told *The New York Times* that he told the infielders in a pregame meeting that Young had a tendency to do. Soriano was out of position, and Randolph couldn't get his attention. First baseman Nick Johnson, seeing Randolph trying to get to Soriano, moved toward

second, stopping Young's smash. The ball glanced off Johnson's glove and to Soriano, who flipped the ball to first to end the game.

Randolph told *The Times* he didn't ask Soriano about the play after the game. He waited until the next day before the former Yankees All-Star let Soriano know, again, that being a complete player includes playing defense.

"When you start talking about the whole package, that's when you see the confidence get to a new level," Randolph told *The Times*. "That's when you start saying: 'I enjoy doing this.'"

The next day, Soriano made his first error of the year. After leading all major-league second basemen with 23 errors in 2002, Soriano not making an error until the 24th game of the year put him at a pace right at his goal of 15 errors or less. Still, it happened at a time when one of the first prolonged slumps of Soriano's career was about to test the young second baseman.

After 16 multi-hit games in April alone, Soriano had 19 multi-hit games in May and June combined. And, he needed four in his last five June games to reach that number.

The four multi-hit games came in four consecutive games, and immediately after, manager Joe Torre benched Soriano for a game. The night before the benching, a June 25 win over Tampa Bay, every Yankees hitter except Soriano had at least one walk. Soriano

OPPOSITE: Alfonso and Derek Jeter take fielding practice.

AP/WWP

went 0-6 with two strikeouts and looked bad on a home run cut that ended up as a swinging bunt.

"Sori looks like he's got one swing right now—trying to hit the ball out of the park," Torre told the *New York Daily News*. "He's probably a little tired. He's missing balls he usually at least fouls back. Sometimes you don't realize you're doing it. That was a sign to me that he's tired."

During the June dip, even the home run eluded Soriano. He went 12 straight games without going deep, his longest drought in over a year. In 2002, Soriano went more than 10 games without a home run only once. That was in the 11-game stretch to end the year when he was trying to turn every pitch into his 40th home run of the season. It was during this 12-game drought that Torre and hitting coach Rick Down began to notice Soriano putting more and more pitches outside the third base line. Because Soriano has such quick wrists, he can get his bat, even though it weighs as much as a tree stump, through the zone quicker than almost any other big leaguer. If that quickness isn't controlled by keeping his shoulders square instead of opening up, Soriano is going to be in front of almost any pitch and will pull everything to left field or foul. Having the bat out in front too quickly means those quick wrists aren't generating much power.

Oakland A's shortstop Miguel Tejada, the 2002 American League MVP, said that in addition to the mechanical problems, a big reason for Soriano's struggles was that he was now seen as a target. For the first time in his career, Soriano was now the focus of game plans, something that Tejada said contributed to his own early-season struggles in 2003.

"Big-league pitchers are smart," Tejada said. "They are going to make their own changes and adjustments. You have a year like Soriano had, and pitchers start looking a little more closely at what you're doing and how to get you out. I've seen it. Pitchers are used to seeing me. They know what I like to do. But that's baseball. If you're a good big-league hitter like he is, you make your own changes to adjust to the changes being thrown at you."

Torre stayed on Soriano most of June about waiting on pitches. In a June 20 game against the Mets at Shea Stadium, Soriano hit a towering third-inning home run to left field off Steve Trachsel. In the fifth, Soriano thought he had another dinger, this time to center field. Tsuyoshi Shinjo reached over the wall and robbed Soriano of his 20th home run. The smash was bittersweet for Torre. He was happy that Soriano had waited on the pitch and drove it to center instead of trying to pull the ball. He wasn't happy that Soriano stood at home plate admiring his handiwork.

Alfonso greets fellow San Pedro de Macoris native Chicago Cubs slugger Sammy Sosa at second base during the Yankees' 2003 matchup with the Cubs.

Ever since his rookie year, Torre has warned Soriano about standing at home plate on deep fly balls. In the 2001 American League Championship Series against Seattle, Soriano thought so much of a deep drive in Game 1 that he barely trotted up the first base line after hitting it. The ball bounced off the wall, Soriano was held to a single, and the Yankee manager was not pleased.

Two years later, the home run expectations have caused Soriano to sometimes forget he's in the leadoff role. The June troubles had the team pulling out their black book and looking for help. Reggie Jackson was brought in to talk to Soriano about being patient at the plate and not trying to turn everything into a highlight reel piece. The Yankees also dipped into *La Cadena*.

When Soriano first arrived on the Yankees scene in 2000, Luis Sojo was still bouncing around the big leagues. Sojo was a familiar face who spoke a familiar language. He helped Soriano get adjusted to life in New York and life as a Yankees player. Though he played little, Sojo, beloved in the Yankees' organization, had been through the big-league trenches. He retired during spring training in 2002, taking on a minor-league managing gig before playing in the Mexican League. Believing Soriano needed another shot of Sojo, the team asked if Sojo would be willing to return to the big club as a special

instructor. Sojo jumped at the opportunity, retiring from the Mexican League and quickly finding the nearest cab to the airport.

The Yankees hadn't had a Hispanic coach since Jose Cardenal's 1999 departure. And even though the team said Sojo's hiring was to help bridge the gap with all Latin American players, it's easy to tell that this *La Cadena* hiring had the second baseman in mind.

Soriano is getting more accustomed to everyday New York life on and off the field. However, he is still fairly new to the United States and to the big-league lifestyle. Closer Mariano Rivera consistently reminds Soriano of his need to continue learning English, something Sojo encourages and something Soriano has improved tremendously. Soriano is now comfortable doing interviews in the language, even if the English is picked up watching almost any DVD he can get his hands on.

"I learned the language by watching TV and by listening and listening," Rivera said. "I always tell the guys that they have to learn the language to be truly successful. If you make the effort and are willing to learn, people will teach you. You have to use everything available to you."

Soriano's bat and his newfound ability to communicate with those who tell his story have made Soriano a Bronx Bombers favorite. Evidently, those things have also made him a national favorite. Soriano earned the American League starting spot at the All-Star Game for the second straight year. He led all American League players in votes in 2003 until the final week of online voting, when all the votes from Japan were finally calculated. And even though Soriano is still a popular player across the pond, he wasn't popular enough to keep Seattle Mariners outfielder Ichiro Suzuki from overtaking him for the overall lead.

The point had been made. Alfonso Soriano had arrived. Yes, he arrived last year with a magical 2002. But the hot start to

AP/WWP

2003 was putting his mug on televisions all over the country and his name on many baseball fans' radar screens. He broke his own Yankees record by reaching 20 home runs and 20 stolen bases in Game 74, nine games quicker than 2002. In the monkey-see/monkey-do baseball world, teams tried to emulate the speed/power combination the Yankees were getting from second base. Several organizations tried what New York did, moving a natural shortstop to second base.

The Texas Rangers moved one of their top prospects, fellow Dominican Ramón Nivar, from his natural home as *la cabeza* to across the diamond. The move was made with visions of Soriano-like production dancing in the Rangers' heads.

"To me," said Nivar, who rewarded the Rangers by leading the AA Texas League in hitting during the league's first half, "Soriano is the second baseman everyone wants to be like. He's the standard right now. He hits for power yet can steal bases, and he hits leadoff. He made the switch from shortstop. He's definitely someone a lot of people would like to be like right now."

Yankees players, coaches, staff, anyone with an interlocking NY on his head, likes to talk about how good Soriano can be. First baseman Jason Giambi has never backed off

believing that Soriano could eventually hit 50 home runs and steal 50 bases. Hitting coaches around the league say you can tell when Soriano is in the batting cage by the sound of the bat. As ESPN's Dave Campbell said, it's Soriano's "electric body" getting those lighting-quick wrists and that big bat wound up.

Randolph is quick to point out that defense and learning how to keep defensive focus in balance with the hitting focus still needs improvement. And Soriano will *eventually* learn that every ball isn't a home run.

Right now, though, it just seems like everything in the life of Alfonso Soriano is that way.

"The guy is already a superstar in the big leagues, and there is no telling how much better he is going to get," said Red Sox pitcher Pedro Martinez, Soriano's countryman and one of the most popular players in the Dominican Republic. "I'll tell you this: He's going to be a mega-star."

In San Pedro de Macoris, Soriano is already at mega-star level. He's beloved in the community and throughout the island. He's in the big leagues. And he's already accomplished the goal he set when he was seven: He bought his mom a new house.

Mission accomplished.

The Dominican dream…come true.

InnerWorkings™

AP/WWP

INNERWORKINGS SALUTES ALFONSO SORIANO!